Final Harvest

EMILY DICKINSON'S
POEMS

Final Harvest

EMILY DICKINSON'S
— POEMS —

SELECTION AND INTRODUCTION BY
Thomas H. Johnson

BOSTON • TORONTO

LITTLE, BROWN AND COMPANY

LIBRARY OF CONGRESS CATALOG CARD NO. 62-8061

Tenth Printing

V

The publisher in presenting this volume acknowledges permission of the
President and Fellows of Harvard College and of the Trustees of Amherst
College.

BP

*Published simultaneously in Canada
by Little, Brown & Company (Canada) Limited*

PRINTED IN THE UNITED STATES OF AMERICA

Biographical Note

EMILY DICKINSON was born in Amherst, Massachusetts, on December 10, 1830, daughter of a respected Amherst lawyer, Edward Dickinson, and his wife Emily Norcross Dickinson. She lived throughout her life in her father's house in Amherst, with her parents (until their deaths in her middle years) and younger sister Lavinia. Her brother William Austin Dickinson and his wife Susan Gilbert Dickinson lived next door.

She was educated in local schools and at Mount Holyoke Female Seminary in South Hadley. Her childhood and girlhood were active and social, but after a trip to Washington and Philadelphia in 1855 she settled into a quiet pattern of life, never leaving Amherst except for two trips (for eye care) to Boston, seeing fewer and fewer people outside her close family circle and old friends, and drawing gradually into seclusion.

She died, after a two-year illness, on May 15, 1886. Except for seven anonymous verses, her poems were unpublished during her lifetime. They were found after her death, and editions of sections of them have appeared over the years since then. A three-volume variorum edition of her complete poems (totaling 1775), derived from all known manuscripts and edited by Thomas H. Johnson, was published in 1955 by Harvard University Press; the standard one-volume edition of the complete poems, derived from the variorum edition and also edited by Mr. Johnson, was published in 1960 by Little, Brown and Company.

The best record of Emily Dickinson's appearance is in one of her letters to Thomas Wentworth Higginson, to whom she had turned as a literary adviser: "I . . . am small, like the wren; and my hair is bold, like the chestnut burr; and my eyes, like the sherry in the glass that the guest leaves."

The Vision and Veto
of Emily Dickinson

W HEN EMILY DICKINSON in 1862 enclosed a handful of
her poems in a letter to the essayist and reformer Thomas
Wentworth Higginson, inquiring whether her verses "breathed," she
received a bewildered response. The man she would thenceforth os-
tensibly make her literary mentor thought their gait "spasmodic," but
he wanted to see more, and asked about her reading. She replied: "For
Poets, I have Keats, and Mr. and Mrs. Browning. For Prose, Mr.
Ruskin, Sir Thomas Browne, and the Revelations." The fragmentary
selection is emblematic not only of the nature of Dickinson herself,
but of her poetry as well, for it both conceals and reveals. The signifi-
cant names, as a study of her poetry amply confirms, are the last two.
Browne's concern with language and his solemn reflections on death
and immortality are the heart of Dickinson's inner world; its soul is
the ecstatic vision of John of Patmos.

Emily Dickinson loved words ardently. Her feeling about them
amounted to veneration and her selection of them was ritualistic. "A
Word made Flesh is seldom/And tremblingly partook," she begins
one poem (no. 1651), and continues: "A Word that breathes dis-
tinctly/Has not the power to die." Is there any act, she asks, more
blessed than the divine descent, the voluntary stooping of immanence,
to reach the ear and heart of the creature, to make the Word live?
Thoughts greatly conceived and expressed have sacramental efficacy.
Almost all the poems touching upon the indwelling glory of language
were written in 1862 and 1863, the years of flood creativeness. One

cannot escape the conviction that she is acknowledging the pervasive force of such inspiration in "The Soul that hath a Guest" (no. 674), one of her noble utterances. "A Word dropped careless on a Page" (no. 1261) breeds infection. Near the end of her life she wrote a close friend: "I hesitate which word to take, as I can take but few and each must be the chiefest, but recall that Earth's most graphic transaction is placed within a syllable, nay, even a gaze." As artist, Dickinson conceived of brevity, not as a way to sketch in miniature, but as a means of achieving the single moment of intensity. Her way of living, her isolation, she adopted out of necessity, for her nature like her poetry combined tenseness with exultation. After Higginson called on her in 1870 he wrote: "I never was with anyone who drained my nerve power so much. Without touching her, she drew from me. I am glad not to live near her."

No one was more aware of the draining effect in personal contacts than Dickinson herself. Her poems expressing the need to be abstemious of friends are thoughts dictated by the forces that possessed her.

> Who never wanted — maddest Joy
> Remains to him unknown —
> The Banquet of Abstemiousness
> Defaces that of Wine —

Clearly she was possessed to a most uncommon degree by emotional responses so acute as to be painful to herself and others. One thus understands why letters increasingly became her chosen medium of communication.

> The Soul selects her own Society —
> Then — shuts the Door —
> To her divine Majority —
> Present no more —

The lines of course name a way of electing friends. But they also imply the frugal doling out of emotions lest their intensity leave one bare and charred.

Emily Dickinson had no formal theory of poetics, but she had a consistent idea of the manner in which the poet is inspired, explicitly set forth in "Alone, I cannot be" (no. 298). Inspiration comes as a grace, overleaping regular channels; the poet is thus (like Keats perhaps) a being possessed, who reveals truth out of the agony of travail; and the anguish of such possession enables the receiver to partake of reality and reveal at least a fragment of the mysteries that the heart perceives.

Uncontrolled, such possession leads into the sheer nonsense of automatic writing, and Dickinson had no more success than any other artist has ever had in giving form to every creative impulse. But her successes, she seems to have felt when she wrote Higginson in 1862, were increasingly evident. She persistently labored to file her lines to sharpen the images. She was aware that form inheres in the created object, and she achieved control when her perceptions gave shape to the object before her pen touched paper.

An example of a failure is her poem about two butterflies (no. 533), in which she seems to have intended to portray their lightness and darting motion. But by the time she reaches the end, her focus is so blurred that the reader has forgotten what she is writing about. She was aware of the failure, and many years later began it over again. But inspiration was not with her. The penciled worksheet draft survives, and is rare in the degree of its complication. She never completed the poem, which remains a fascinating document of poetic creativeness in travail.

On one occasion, however, the muse sustained her in a similar attempt. She wished, sometime about 1862, to sketch the portrait of a hummingbird. She sees a vibration and hears a whir so rapid that only the stir of blossoms after the bird's departure assures her of the truth of its presence. But the lines of "Within my Garden, rides a Bird" (no. 500) have been assembled laboriously and the figures remain awkward: the bird praises, and the rejoined dog is perplexed whether

[ix]

he too (or the poet?) saw the bird. She never forgot what she wanted to express about the hummingbird, as sound, iridescent color, vibration; as instantaneous translation through space. Some eighteen years later she returned to the theme, reduced the twenty lines to eight, and created the superb poem about "A Route of Evanescence" (no. 1463), a creation which seems to have sprung fully armed from the brow of Jove. A similar achievement is the poem depicting frost, "A Visitor in Marl" (no. 391); and in it seems to coalesce all the virtuosity so signally her own: the wit of the keen phrase, brevity, and exact focus.

"If I read a book," she told Higginson, "and it makes my whole body so cold no fire ever can warm me, I know *that* is poetry. If I feel physically as if the top of my head were taken off, I know *that* is poetry. These are the only ways I know it. Is there any other way?" To be sure there are other ways that poetry may be known, but there was no other way that she could successfully write it. One does not imagine that such masterpieces as *Lycidas* or *Alexander's Feast* were the performances of men who felt the top of their heads being taken off. Yet the end in view for Dickinson, as it had been for Milton and Dryden, was the creation of a work of art wherein the form and idea are one. Robert Frost has expressed the concept thus: "Like a piece of ice on a hot stove, the poem must ride on its own melting."

There is a further prospect from which Emily Dickinson's way of writing poetry may be viewed. Like many poets, during a period of composition Shelley set himself the task of writing a certain number of lines which he thereafter polished. Such poets visualize in panorama. They conceive spatially and wish to convey readers over expanse. Chaucer, Keats, and Byron expressed themselves notably in narrative poems. Dickinson on occasion tried to write narratively, but her genius was of a different order, and the few such poems that she wrote communicate at a pedestrian level. She is much more akin to such seventeenth-century poets as Donne, Vaughan, and Marvell in her ability to make the word itself become flesh, and she concentrated her effort to such a degree that she rarely wrote a poem of more than twenty lines. Her longest is fifty lines: "I cannot live with You" (no. 640).

As a prosodist experimenting in meters, rhyme, capitals, grammar, and punctuation, Emily Dickinson exhibited a boldness which doomed her to obscurity in her lifetime. Yet the stature she continues to take, merely as a technician, is notable in the history of literary reputations, and the full penetration of her accomplishment as a virtuoso is still a venture. Her manner of writing helps give assurance of the infinite adaptability of language. An innovator is of necessity unorthodox, and Dickinson's syntax forces the reader to unexpected levels of concept. She used dashes as a musical device and capital letters as a means of emphasis. Her readers are now gradually accommodating themselves to such eccentricities, since they know they are inheriting the legacy of a private poet who deliberately fractured grammar to achieve special effects. Indeed, an extraordinary achievement in the use of syntax to imply a meaning beyond the logic of relationships is the seventeen-line poem "I like to see it lap the Miles" (no. 585). Apparently it celebrates that exciting new form of transportation, the railroad. In structure it is but one sentence with a single subject and predicate (the first two words), which draw behind them an iron horse in a series of objective complements: *lap, lick, stop, step, peer, pare, crawl, chase, neigh, stop.* This happy journey is conducted without passengers; in fact the toy comes back to "its own stable door" at the end of its brief circuit. The satire on "progress" is the more biting in that it is masked by a child-like enthusiasm.

But the chief contribution of Dickinson to English prosody was the extension she gave to metrical and rhyme patterns. Her meters she derived from the hymn-book measures of her day,* adapted to her own requirements of suppleness and variety, retardment and acceleration. To exact rhymes and eye-rhymes (*come-home*), considered the only pairings allowable in English verse, she adds the constant use of identical rhymes (*stone-stone*), vowel rhymes (*see-buy*), imperfect rhymes (*time-thine*), and suspended rhymes (*thing-along*). The flexibility thus gained enormously extends the range of variations and creates rich overtones. For example, "We play at Paste" (no. 320), a poem of

* These I have discussed in detail in *Emily Dickinson: An Interpretive Biography* (1955), pages 84-86.

[xi]

two quatrains, uses three varieties of rhyme: identical, suspended, and exact. The idea of the poem juxtaposes the tyro and the artist, and the form does likewise. The alternate iambic dimeter-trimeter regularity of the first stanza is abandoned in the second, where the meter follows its own convention, striking out in a new direction. Most interesting are the two final lines. The thought of line seven concerns the artist whose craft is mastered; that of line eight, the learner. The metric patterns of the two lines enforce the thought by reversing the beat ($\cup - - \cup \mid - \cup \cup -$) and the hovering rhyme at the start alters to exact rhyme at the conclusion. This is but one among scores of poems in which the poet makes form and meaning inhere.

But it is not her achievement as a prosodist, substantial as it is, that gives high rank to Emily Dickinson. It is her tragic vision. She knew that she could not pierce through to the unknowable, but she insisted on asking the questions. Her agonizing sense of ironic contrasts; of the weight of suffering; of the human predicament in which man is mocked, destroyed, and beckoned to some incomprehensible repose; of the limits of reason, order, and justice in human as well as divine relationships: — this is the anguish of the Shakespeare of *King Lear*, and it was shared in like degree among nineteenth-century American writers only by Herman Melville, who also had his war with God. Yet, unlike Melville, she is willing to love the God with whom she is at war. Thus she is a closer spiritual neighbor to Jonathan Edwards, who believed (as she evidently did) that final judgment is not a foreseeable end, but a pronouncement renewed in all moments of existence.

Late in her life the death of her cherished eight-year-old nephew drew from her this moving statement, a summation in fact of her philosophy:

'Open the Door, open the Door, they are waiting for me,' was Gilbert's sweet command in delirium. *Who* were waiting for him, all we possess we would give to know — Anguish at last opened it, and he ran to the little Grave at his Grandparents' feet — All this and more, though *is* there more? More than Love and Death? Then tell me its name!

Emily Dickinson was an existentialist in a period of transcendentalism, a movement in her New England which saw the immanence of God in a buttercup, a state which she once or twice in poetry tried to envision. Yet her judgment persistently asserts that neither intuition nor reason can solve the riddle of existence, and in her lifetime only the actress Eleonora Duse lived with a similar artistic effectiveness for audiences. Dickinson assesses the problems of anxiety and loneliness, the extremity of pain and its duration and redemptive quality, and she thereby steadily participated in the issues of existing. "More than Love and Death?"

Her quest always involves time-theme ambiguities among the many paradoxes, and as a poet she adopts a variety of masks. There was the mask of little-girlhood, which gave her freedom to make such social commentary as "I like to see it lap the Miles." Her signature "Your Scholar" in her letters to Higginson followed a creative maturity which she knew he did not fathom. The mask hid the tragic vision in such patent mockery as "How happy is the little Stone" (no. 1510), and it gave her deeply religious nature the appearance of unorthodoxy. It was adopted in her whim of dressing in white and remaining physically out of sight of visitors. (Late in life she wrote to a new acquaintance: "In all the circumference of Expression, those guileless words of Adam and Eve never were surpassed, 'I was afraid and hid Myself.'") It appears consummately in such poems as "Title divine — is mine" (no. 1072), and "Mine — by the Right of the White Election" (no. 528), which seem intended to express both an earthly-heavenly marriage, and the agony of one who inevitably accepts the fact that a much desired human tie must be renounced: "Mine — here — in Vision — and in Veto!"

The subterranean vehemence of such poems as "Fame of Myself, to justify" (no. 713) and "Publication — is the Auction/Of the Mind of Man" (no. 709), written after she was convinced that during her lifetime there would be no prospect of sharing her way of writing in any public way, suggests renunciation at another level. Love and Death! By placing "Because I could not stop for Death" (no. 712) beside "Behind Me — dips Eternity" (no. 721), one experiences the range of both her mortal consciousness and her beatific vision.

Publisher's Note

THE POEMS in this selection are numbered consecutively. The second number (in parentheses) is the number of the poem in *The Complete Poems of Emily Dickinson*.

The date at the left following each poem is that conjectured for the earliest known manuscript of the poem. That at the right is the date when the poem was first published.

Contents

Final Harvest

EMILY DICKINSON'S
POEMS

The feet of people walking home
With gayer sandals go –
The Crocus – till she rises
The Vassal of the snow –
The lips at Hallelujah
Long years of practise bore
Till bye and bye these Bargemen
Walked singing on the shore.

Pearls are the Diver's farthings
Extorted from the Sea –
Pinions – the Seraph's wagon
Pedestrian once – as we –
Night is the morning's Canvas
Larceny – legacy –
Death, but our rapt attention
To Immortality.

My figures fail to tell me
How far the Village lies –
Whose peasants are the Angels –
Whose Cantons dot the skies –
My Classics veil their faces –
My faith that Dark adores –
Which from its solemn abbeys
Such resurrection pours.

c. 1858   1914

I never told the buried gold
Upon the hill – that lies –
I saw the sun – his plunder done
Crouch low to guard his prize.

He stood as near
As stood you here –
A pace had been between –
Did but a snake bisect the brake
My life had forfeit been.

That was a wondrous booty –
I hope 'twas honest gained.
Those were the fairest ingots
That ever kissed the spade!

Whether to keep the secret –
Whether to reveal –
Whether as I ponder
Kidd will sudden sail –

Could a shrewd advise me
We might e'en divide –
Should a shrewd betray me –
Atropos decide!

c. 1858   *1914*

The morns are meeker than they were –
The nuts are getting brown –
The berry's cheek is plumper –
The Rose is out of town.

The Maple wears a gayer scarf –
The field a scarlet gown –
Lest I should be old fashioned
I'll put a trinket on.

c. *1858*   *1890*

4
(18)

The Gentian weaves her fringes –
The Maple's loom is red –
My departing blossoms
    Obviate parade.

A brief, but patient illness –
An hour to prepare,
And one below this morning
Is where the angels are –
It was a short procession,
The Bobolink was there –
An aged Bee addressed us –
And then we knelt in prayer –
We trust that she was willing –
We ask that we may be.
Summer – Sister – Seraph!
Let us go with thee!

In the name of the Bee –
And of the Butterfly –
And of the Breeze – Amen!

c. *1858*   *1891*

[3]

I had a guinea golden –
I lost it in the sand –
And tho' the sum was simple
And pounds were in the land –
Still, had it such a value
Unto my frugal eye –
That when I could not find it –
I sat me down to sigh.

I had a crimson Robin –
Who sang full many a day
But when the woods were painted,
He, too, did fly away –
Time brought me other Robins –
Their ballads were the same –
Still, for my missing Troubadour
I kept the "house at hame."

I had a star in heaven –
One "Pleiad" was its name –
And when I was not heeding,
It wandered from the same.
And tho' the skies are crowded –
And all the night ashine –
I do not care about it –
Since none of them are mine.

My story has a moral –
I have a missing friend –
"Pleiad" its name, and Robin,
And guinea in the sand.
And when this mournful ditty
Accompanied with tear –

[4]

Shall meet the eye of traitor
In country far from here –
Grant that repentance solemn
May seize upon his mind –
And he no consolation
Beneath the sun may find.

c. 1858   *1896*

6
(47)

Heart! We will forget him!
You and I – tonight!
You may forget the warmth he gave –
I will forget the light!

When you have done, pray tell me
That I may straight begin!
Haste! lest while you're lagging
I remember him!

c. 1858   *1896*

7
(49)

I never lost as much but twice,
And that was in the sod.
Twice have I stood a beggar
Before the door of God!

Angels – twice descending
Reimbursed my store –
Burglar! Banker – Father!
I am poor once more!

c. 1858   *1890*

[5]

o
(55)
By Chivalries as tiny,
A Blossom, or a Book,
The seeds of smiles are planted –
Which blossom in the dark.

1858   *1945*

9
(59)
A little East of Jordan,
Evangelists record,
A Gymnast and an Angel
Did wrestle long and hard –

Till morning touching mountain –
And Jacob, waxing strong,
The Angel begged permission
To Breakfast – to return –

Not so, said cunning Jacob!
"I will not let thee go
Except thou bless me" – Stranger!
The which acceded to –

Light swung the silver fleeces
"Peniel" Hills beyond,
And the bewildered Gymnast
Found he had worsted God!

c. 1859   *1914*

[6]

Papa above!
Regard a Mouse
O'erpowered by the Cat!
Reserve within thy kingdom
A "Mansion" for the Rat!

Snug in seraphic Cupboards
To nibble all the day,
While unsuspecting Cycles
Wheel solemnly away!

c. *1859*   *1914*

Success is counted sweetest
By those who ne'er succeed.
To comprehend a nectar
Requires sorest need.

Not one of all the purple Host
Who took the Flag today
Can tell the definition
So clear of Victory

As he defeated – dying –
On whose forbidden ear
The distant strains of triumph
Burst agonized and clear!

c. *1859*   *1878*

12
(69)
Low at my problem bending,
Another problem comes –
Larger than mine – Serener –
Involving statelier sums.

I check my busy pencil,
My figures file away.
Wherefore, my baffled fingers
Thy perplexity?

1859   *1914*

13
(75)
She died at play,
Gambolled away
Her lease of spotted hours,
Then sank as gaily as a Turk
Upon a Couch of flowers.

Her ghost strolled softly o'er the hill
Yesterday, and Today,
Her vestments as the silver fleece –
Her countenance as spray.

c. 1859   *1914*

14
(76)
Exultation is the going
Of an inland soul to sea,

[8]

Past the houses – past the headlands –
Into deep Eternity –

Bred as we, among the mountains,
Can the sailor understand
The divine intoxication
Of the first league out from land?

c. *1859*   *1890*

15
(89)

Some things that fly there be –
Birds – Hours – the Bumblebee –
Of these no Elegy.

Some things that stay there be –
Grief – Hills – Eternity –
Nor this behooveth me.

There are that resting, rise.
Can I expound the skies?
How still the Riddle lies!

c. *1859*   *1890*

16
(98)

One dignity delays for all –
One mitred Afternoon –
None can avoid this purple –
None evade this Crown!

Coach, it insures, and footmen –
Chamber, and state, and throng –

Bells, also, in the village
As we ride grand along!

What dignified Attendants!
What service when we pause!
How loyally at parting
Their hundred hats they raise!

How pomp surpassing ermine
When simple You, and I,
Present our meek escutcheon
And claim the rank to die!

c. 1859   *1890*

17
(105)
To hang our head – ostensibly –
And subsequent, to find
That such was not the posture
Of our immortal mind –

Affords the sly presumption
That in so dense a fuzz –
You – too – take Cobweb attitudes
Upon a plane of Gauze!

c. 1859

18
(113)
Our share of night to bear –
Our share of morning –

[10]

Our blank in bliss to fill
Our blank in scorning –

Here a star, and there a star,
Some lose their way!
Here a mist, and there a mist,
Afterwards – Day!

c. 1859   *1890*

19
(115)

What Inn is this
Where for the night
Peculiar Traveller comes?
Who is the Landlord?
Where the maids?
Behold, what curious rooms!
No ruddy fires on the hearth –
No brimming Tankards flow –
Necromancer! Landlord!
Who are these below?

c. 1859   *1891*

20
(125)

For each ecstatic instant
We must an anguish pay
In keen and quivering ratio
To the ecstasy.

For each beloved hour
Sharp pittances of years –

[11]

Bitter contested farthings –
And Coffers heaped with Tears!

c. 1859

1891

21
(126)
To fight aloud, is very brave –
But *gallanter*, I know
Who charge within the bosom
The Cavalry of Woe –

Who win, and nations do not see –
Who fall – and none observe –
Whose dying eyes, no Country
Regards with patriot love –

We trust, in plumed procession
For such, the Angels go –
Rank after Rank, with even feet –
And Uniforms of Snow.

c. 1859

1890

22
(128)
Bring me the sunset in a cup,
Reckon the morning's flagons up
And say how many Dew,
Tell me how far the morning leaps –
Tell me what time the weaver sleeps
Who spun the breadths of blue!

Write me how many notes there be
In the new Robin's ecstasy
Among astonished boughs –
How many trips the Tortoise makes –
How many cups the Bee partakes,
The Debauchee of Dews!

Also, who laid the Rainbow's piers,
Also, who leads the docile spheres
By withes of supple blue?
Whose fingers string the stalactite –
Who counts the wampum of the night
To see that none is due?

Who built this little Alban House
And shut the windows down so close
My spirit cannot see?
Who'll let me out some gala day
With implements to fly away,
Passing Pomposity?

c. 1859   *1891*

23
(130)
These are the days when Birds come back –
A very few – a Bird or two –
To take a backward look.

These are the days when skies resume
The old – old sophistries of June –
A blue and gold mistake.

Oh fraud that cannot cheat the Bee –
Almost thy plausibility
Induces my belief.

[13]

Till ranks of seeds their witness bear –
And softly thro' the altered air
Hurries a timid leaf.

Oh Sacrament of summer days,
Oh Last Communion in the Haze –
Permit a child to join.

Thy sacred emblems to partake –
Thy consecrated bread to take
And thine immortal wine!

c. 1859   *1890*

24
(131)

Besides the Autumn poets sing
A few prosaic days
A little this side of the snow
And that side of the Haze –

A few incisive Mornings –
A few Ascetic Eves –
Gone – Mr. Bryant's "Golden Rod" –
And Mr. Thomson's "sheaves."

Still, is the bustle in the Brook –
Sealed are the spicy valves –
Mesmeric fingers softly touch
The Eyes of many Elves –

Perhaps a squirrel may remain –
My sentiments to share –
Grant me, Oh Lord, a sunny mind –
Thy windy will to bear!

c. 1859   *1891*

25
(140)
An altered look about the hills –
A Tyrian light the village fills –
A wider sunrise in the morn –
A deeper twilight on the lawn –
A print of a vermillion foot –
A purple finger on the slope –
A flippant fly upon the pane –
A spider at his trade again –
An added strut in Chanticleer –
A flower expected everywhere –
An axe shrill singing in the woods –
Fern odors on untravelled roads –
All this and more I cannot tell –
A furtive look you know as well –
And Nicodemus' Mystery
Receives its annual reply!

c. 1859

1891

26
(153)
Dust is the only Secret –
Death, the only One
You cannot find out all about
In his "native town."

Nobody knew "his Father" –
Never was a Boy –
Hadn't any playmates,
Or "Early history" –

Industrious! Laconic!
Punctual! Sedate!

[15]

Bold as a Brigand!
Stiller than a Fleet!

Builds, like a Bird, too!
Christ robs the Nest –
Robin after Robin
Smuggled to Rest!

c. 1860   *1914*

27
(160)

Just lost, when I was saved!
Just felt the world go by!
Just girt me for the onset with Eternity,
When breath blew back,
And on the other side
I heard recede the disappointed tide!

Therefore, as One returned, I feel
Odd secrets of the line to tell!
Some Sailor, skirting foreign shores –
Some pale Reporter, from the awful doors
Before the Seal!

Next time, to stay!
Next time, the things to see
By Ear unheard,
Unscrutinized by Eye –

Next time, to tarry,
While the Ages steal –
Slow tramp the Centuries,
And the Cycles wheel!

c. 1860   *1891*

28
(165)
A *Wounded* Deer – leaps highest –
I've heard the Hunter tell –
'Tis but the Ecstasy of *death* –
And then the Brake is still!

The *Smitten* Rock that gushes!
The *trampled* Steel that springs!
A Cheek is always redder
Just where the Hectic stings!

Mirth is the Mail of Anguish –
In which it Cautious Arm,
Lest anybody spy the blood
And "you're hurt" exclaim!

c. 1860   *1890*

29
(167)
To learn the Transport by the Pain –
As Blind Men learn the sun!
To die of thirst – suspecting
That Brooks in Meadows run!

To stay the homesick – homesick feet
Upon a foreign shore –
Haunted by native lands, the while –
And blue – beloved air!

This is the Sovereign Anguish!
This – the signal woe!
These are the patient "Laureates"
Whose voices – trained – below –

[17]

Ascend in ceaseless Carol –
Inaudible, indeed,
To us – the duller scholars
Of the Mysterious Bard!

c. 1860   *1891*

30
(174)

At last, to be identified!
At last, the lamps upon thy side
The rest of Life to *see*!

Past Midnight! Past the Morning Star!
Past Sunrise!
Ah, What leagues there *were*
Between our feet, and Day!

c. 1860   *1890*

31
(178)

I cautious, scanned my little life –
I winnowed what would fade
From what would last till Heads like mine
Should be a-dreaming laid.

I put the latter in a Barn –
The former, blew away.
I went one winter morning
And lo – my priceless Hay

Was not upon the "Scaffold" –
Was not upon the "Beam" –

And from a thriving Farmer –
A Cynic, I became.

Whether a Thief did it –
Whether it was the wind –
Whether Deity's guiltless –
My business is, to find!

So I begin to ransack!
How is it Hearts, with Thee?
Art thou within the little Barn
Love provided Thee?

c. 1860   1929

32
(182)
If I shouldn't be alive
When the Robins come,
Give the one in Red Cravat,
A Memorial crumb.

If I couldn't thank you,
Being fast asleep,
You will know I'm trying
With my Granite lip!

c. 1860   1890

33
(184)
A transport one cannot contain
May yet a transport be –

[19]

Though God forbid it lift the lid –
Unto its Ecstasy!

A Diagram – of Rapture!
A sixpence at a Show –
With Holy Ghosts in Cages!
The *Universe* would go!

c. *1860*   *1935*

34
(185)
"Faith" is a fine invention
When Gentlemen can *see* –
But *Microscopes* are prudent
In an Emergency.

c. *1860*   *1891*

35
(187)
How many times these low feet staggered –
Only the soldered mouth can tell –
Try – can you stir the awful rivet –
Try – can you lift the hasps of steel!

Stroke the cool forehead – hot so often –
Lift – if you care – the listless hair –
Handle the adamantine fingers
Never a thimble – more – shall wear –

Buzz the dull flies – on the chamber window –
Brave – shines the sun through the freckled pane –

[20]

Fearless – the cobweb swings from the ceiling –
Indolent Housewife – in Daisies – lain!

c. 1860   *1890*

36
(189)

It's such a little thing to weep –
So short a thing to sigh –
And yet – by Trades – the size of *these*
We men and women die!

c. 1860   *1896*

37
(193)

I shall know why – when Time is over –
And I have ceased to wonder why –
Christ will explain each separate anguish
In the fair schoolroom of the sky –

He will tell me what "Peter" promised –
And I – for wonder at his woe –
I shall forget the drop of Anguish
That scalds me now – that scalds me now!

c. 1860   *1890*

38
(195)

For this – accepted Breath –
Through it – compete with Death –
The fellow cannot touch this Crown –

[21]

By it – my title take –
Ah, what a royal sake
To my necessity – stooped down!

No Wilderness – can be
Where this attendeth me –
No Desert Noon –
No fear of frost to come
Haunt the perennial bloom –
But Certain June!

Get Gabriel – to tell – the royal syllable –
Get Saints – with new – unsteady tongue –
To say what trance below
Most like their glory show –
Fittest the Crown!

c. 1860   1935

39
(199)

I'm "wife" – I've finished that –
That other state –
I'm Czar – I'm "Woman" now –
It's safer so –

How odd the Girl's life looks
Behind this soft Eclipse –
I think that Earth feels so
To folks in Heaven – now –

This being comfort – then
That other kind – was pain –
But why compare?
I'm "Wife"! Stop there!

c. 1860   1890

40
(204)

A slash of Blue –
A sweep of Gray –
Some scarlet patches on the way,
Compose an Evening Sky –
A little purple – slipped between –
Some Ruby Trousers hurried on –
A Wave of Gold –
A Bank of Day –
This just makes out the Morning Sky.

c. 1860   1935

41
(207)

Tho' I get home how late – how late –
So I get home – 'twill compensate –
Better will be the Ecstasy
That they have done expecting me –
When Night – descending – dumb – and dark –
They hear my unexpected knock –
Transporting must the moment be –
Brewed from decades of Agony!

To think just how the fire will burn –
Just how long-cheated eyes will turn –
To wonder what myself will say,
And what itself, will say to me –
Beguiles the Centuries of way!

c. 1860   1891

42
(209)

With thee, in the Desert –
With thee in the thirst –
With thee in the Tamarind wood –
Leopard breathes – at last!

c 1860   1945

43
(210)

The thought beneath so slight a film -
Is more distinctly seen –
As laces just reveal the surge –
Or Mists – the Apennine

c. 1860   1891

44
(211)

Come slowly – Eden!
Lips unused to Thee –
Bashful – sip thy Jessamines -
As the fainting Bee –

Reaching late his flower,
Round her chamber hums –
Counts his nectars –
Enters – and is lost in Balms.

c. 1860   1890

[24]

Did the Harebell loose her girdle
To the lover Bee
Would the Bee the Harebell *hallow*
Much as formerly?

Did the "Paradise" – persuaded –
Yield her moat of pearl –
Would the Eden *be* an Eden,
Or the Earl – an *Earl?*

c. *1860*   *1891*

46
(214)
I taste a liquor never brewed –
From Tankards scooped in Pearl –
Not all the Vats upon the Rhine
Yield such an Alcohol!

Inebriate of Air – am I –
And Debauchee of Dew –
Reeling – thro endless summer days –
From inns of Molten Blue –

When "Landlords" turn the drunken Bee
Out of the Foxglove's door –
When Butterflies – renounce their "drams" –
I shall but drink the more!

Till Seraphs swing their snowy Hats –
And Saints – to windows run –
To see the little Tippler
Leaning against the – Sun –

c. *1860*   *1861*

Safe in their Alabaster Chambers –
Untouched by Morning
And untouched by Noon –
Sleep the meek members of the Resurrection –
Rafter of satin,
And Roof of stone.

Light laughs the breeze
In her Castle above them –
Babbles the Bee in a stolid Ear,
Pipe the Sweet Birds in ignorant cadence –
Ah, what sagacity perished here!

version of 1859   *1862*

Safe in their Alabaster Chambers –
Untouched by Morning –
And untouched by Noon –
Lie the meek members of the Resurrection –
Rafter of Satin – and Roof of Stone!

Grand go the Years – in the Crescent – above them –
Worlds scoop their Arcs –
And Firmaments – row –
Diadems – drop – and Doges – surrender –
Soundless as dots – on a Disc of Snow –

version of 1861   *1890*

48
(217)
Savior! I've no one else to tell –
And so I trouble *thee*.

[26]

I am the one forgot thee so –
Dost thou remember me?
Nor, for myself, I came so far –
That were the little load –
I brought thee the imperial Heart
I had not strength to hold –
The Heart I carried in my own –
Till mine too heavy grew –
Yet – strangest – *heavier* since it went –
Is it too large for *you?*

1861   *1929*

49
(219)

She sweeps with many-colored Brooms –
And leaves the Shreds behind –
Oh Housewife in the Evening West –
Come back, and dust the Pond!

You dropped a Purple Ravelling in –
You dropped an Amber thread –
And now you've littered all the East
With Duds of Emerald!

And still, she plies her spotted Brooms,
And still the Aprons fly,
Till Brooms fade softly into stars –
And then I come away –

c. 1861   *1891*

50
(225)
Jesus! thy Crucifix
Enable thee to guess
The smaller size!

Jesus! thy second face
Mind thee in Paradise
Of ours!

c. *1861*   *1945*

51
(228)
Blazing in Gold and quenching in Purple
Leaping like Leopards to the Sky
Then at the feet of the old Horizon
Laying her spotted Face to die
Stooping as low as the Otter's Window
Touching the Roof and tinting the Barn
Kissing her Bonnet to the Meadow
And the Juggler of Day is gone

c. 1861   *1864*

52
(230)
We – Bee and I – live by the quaffing –
'Tisn't *all Hock* – with us –
Life has its *Ale* –
But it's many a lay of the Dim Burgundy –
We chant – for cheer – when the Wines – fail –

[28]

Do we "get drunk"?
Ask the jolly Clovers!
Do we "beat" our "Wife"?
I – never wed –
Bee – pledges *his* – in minute flagons –
Dainty – as the tress – on her deft Head –

While runs the Rhine –
He and I – revel –
First – at the vat – and latest at the Vine –
Noon – our last Cup –
"Found dead" – "of Nectar" –
By a humming Coroner –
In a By-Thyme!

c. 1861   *1929*

53
(233)

The Lamp burns sure – within –
Tho' Serfs – supply the Oil –
It matters not the busy Wick –
At her phosphoric toil!

The Slave – forgets – to fill –
The Lamp – burns golden – on –
Unconscious that the oil is out –
As that the Slave – is gone.

c. 1861   *1935*

54
(241)

I like a look of Agony,
Because I know it's true –

[29]

Men do not sham Convulsion,
Nor simulate, a Throe –

The Eyes glaze once – and that is Death –
Impossible to feign
The Beads upon the Forehead
By homely Anguish strung.

c. 1861

1890

55
(243)
I've known a Heaven, like a Tent –
To wrap its shining Yards –
Pluck up its stakes, and disappear –
Without the sound of Boards
Or Rip of Nail – Or Carpenter –
But just the miles of Stare –
That signalize a Show's Retreat –
In North America –

No Trace – no Figment of the Thing
That dazzled, Yesterday,
No Ring – no Marvel –
Men, and Feats –
Dissolved as utterly –
As Bird's far Navigation
Discloses just a Hue –
A plash of Oars, a Gaiety –
Then swallowed up, of View.

c. 1861

1929

56
(245)
I held a Jewel in my fingers –
And went to sleep –
The day was warm, and winds were prosy –
I said " 'Twill keep" –

I woke – and chid my honest fingers,
The Gem was gone –
And now, an Amethyst remembrance
Is all I own –

c. 1861   1891

57
(246)
Forever at His side to walk –
The smaller of the two!
Brain of His Brain –
Blood of His Blood –
Two lives – One Being – now –

Forever of His fate to taste –
If grief – the largest part –
If joy – to put my piece away
For that beloved Heart –

All life – to know each other –
Whom we can never learn –
And bye and bye – a Change –
Called Heaven –
Rapt Neighborhoods of Men –
Just finding out – what puzzled us –
Without the lexicon!

c. 1861   1929

[31]

58
(249)

Wild Nights – Wild Nights!
Were I with thee
Wild Nights should be
Our luxury!

Futile – the Winds –
To a Heart in port –
Done with the Compass –
Done with the Chart!

Rowing in Eden –
Ah, the Sea!
Might I but moor – Tonight –
In Thee!

c. *1861*   *1891*

59
(250)

I shall keep singing!
Birds will pass me
On their way to Yellower Climes –
Each – with a Robin's expectation –
I – with my Redbreast –
And my Rhymes –

Late – when I take my place in summer –
But – I shall bring a fuller tune –
Vespers – are sweeter than Matins – Signor –
Morning – only the seed of Noon –

c. *1861*   *1935*

60

(251)

Over the fence –
Strawberries – grow –
Over the fence –
I could climb – if I tried, I know –
Berries are nice!

But – if I stained my Apron –
God would certainly scold!
Oh, dear, – I guess if He were a Boy –
He'd – climb – if He could!

c. 1861   *1945*

61

(252)

I can wade Grief –
Whole Pools of it –
I'm used to that –
But the least push of Joy
Breaks up my feet –
And I tip – drunken –
Let no Pebble – smile –
'Twas the New Liquor –
That was all!

Power is only Pain –
Stranded, thro' Discipline,
Till Weights – will hang –
Give Balm – to Giants –
And they'll wilt, like Men –
Give Himmaleh –
They'll Carry – Him!

c. 1861   *1891*

62

You see I cannot see – your lifetime –
I must guess –
How many times it ache for me – today – Confess –
How many times for my far sake
The brave eyes film –
But I guess guessing hurts –
Mine – get so dim!

Too vague – the face –
My own – so patient – covers –
Too far – the strength –
My timidness enfolds –
Haunting the Heart –
Like her translated faces –
Teasing the want –
It – only – can suffice!

c. 1861   *1929*

63

"Hope" is the thing with feathers –
That perches in the soul –
And sings the tune without the words –
And never stops – at all –

And sweetest – in the Gale – is heard –
And sore must be the storm –
That could abash the little Bird
That kept so many warm –

I've heard it in the chillest land –
And on the strangest Sea –

Yet, never, in Extremity,
It asked a crumb – of Me.

c *1861*   *1891*

64
(255)

To die – takes just a little while –
They say it doesn't hurt –
It's only fainter – by degrees –
And then – it's out of sight –

A darker Ribbon – for a Day –
A Crape upon the Hat –
And then the pretty sunshine comes –
And helps us to forget –

The absent – mystic – creature –
That but for love of us –
Had gone to sleep – that soundest time –
Without the weariness –

c *1861*   *1935*

65
(257)

Delight is as the flight –
Or in the Ratio of it,
As the Schools would say –
The Rainbow's way –
A Skein
Flung colored, after Rain,
Would suit as bright,
Except that flight
Were Aliment –

[35]

"If it would last"
I asked the East,
When that Bent Stripe
Struck up my childish
Firmament –
And I, for glee,
Took Rainbows, as the common way,
And empty Skies
The Eccentricity –

And so with Lives –
And so with Butterflies –
Seen magic – through the fright
That they will cheat the sight –
And Dower latitudes far on –
Some sudden morn –
Our portion – in the fashion –
Done –

c. 1861   1929

66
(258)

There's a certain Slant of light,
Winter Afternoons –
That oppresses, like the Heft
Of Cathedral Tunes –

Heavenly Hurt, it gives us –
We can find no scar,
But internal difference,
Where the Meanings, are –

None may teach it – Any –
'Tis the Seal Despair –
An imperial affliction
Sent us of the Air –

When it comes, the Landscape listens –
Shadows – hold their breath –
When it goes, 'tis like the Distance
On the look of Death –

c. 1861   *1890*

67
(259)

Good Night! Which put the Candle out?
A jealous Zephyr – not a doubt –
Ah, friend, you little knew
How long at that celestial wick
The Angels – labored diligent –
Extinguished – now – for you!

It might – have been the Light House spark –
Some Sailor – rowing in the Dark –
Had importuned to see!
It might – have been the waning lamp
That lit the Drummer from the Camp
To purer Reveille!

c. 1861   *1891*

68
(261)

Put up my lute!
What of – my Music!
Since the sole ear I cared to charm –

Passive – as Granite – laps My Music –
Sobbing – will suit – as well as psalm!

Would but the "Memnon" of the Desert –
Teach me the strain
That vanquished Him –
When He – surrendered to the Sunrise –
Maybe – that – would awaken – them!

c. 1861   *1935*

69
(262)

The lonesome for they know not What –
The Eastern Exiles – be –
Who strayed beyond the Amber line
Some madder Holiday –

And ever since – the purple Moat
They strive to climb – in vain –
As Birds – that tumble from the clouds
Do fumble at the strain –

The Blessed Ether – taught them –
Some Transatlantic Morn –
When Heaven – was too common – to miss –
Too sure – to dote upon!

c. 1861   *1929*

70
(264)

A Weight with Needles on the pounds –
To push, and pierce, besides –

[38]

That if the Flesh resist the Heft –
The puncture – coolly tries –

That not a pore be overlooked
Of all this Compound Frame –
As manifold for Anguish –
As Species – be – for name –

c. 1861   *1935*

71
(266)

This – is the land – the Sunset washes –
These – are the Banks of the Yellow Sea –
Where it rose – or whither it rushes –
These – are the Western Mystery!

Night after Night
Her purple traffic
Strews the landing with Opal Bales –
Merchantmen – poise upon Horizons –
Dip – and vanish like Orioles!

c. 1861   *1890*

72
(268)

Me, change! Me, alter!
Then I will, when on the Everlasting Hill
A Smaller **Purple** grows –

[39]

At sunset, or a lesser glow
Flickers upon Cordillera –
At Day's superior close!

c. *1861*   *1945*

73
(269)

Bound – a trouble –
And lives can bear it!
Limit – how deep a bleeding go!
So – many – drops – of vital scarlet –
Deal with the soul
As with Algebra!

Tell it the Ages – to a cypher –
And it will ache – contented – on –
Sing – at its pain – as any Workman –
Notching the fall of the Even Sun!

c. *1861*   *1935*

74
(272)

I breathed enough to take the Trick –
And now, removed from Air –
I simulate the Breath, so well –
That One, to be quite sure –

The Lungs are stirless – must descend
Among the Cunning Cells –
And touch the Pantomime – Himself,
How numb, the Bellows feels!

c. *1861*   *1896*

75
(276)

Many a phrase has the English language –
I have heard but one –
Low as the laughter of the Cricket,
Loud, as the Thunder's Tongue –

Murmuring, like old Caspian Choirs,
When the Tide's a' lull –
Saying itself in new inflection –
Like a Whippoorwill –

Breaking in bright Orthography
On my simple sleep –
Thundering its Prospective –
Till I stir, and weep –

Not for the Sorrow, done me –
But the push of Joy –
Say it again, Saxon!
Hush – Only to me!

c. 1861   1935

76
(278)

A shady friend – for Torrid days –
Is easier to find –
Than one of higher temperature
For Frigid – hour of Mind –

The Vane a little to the East –
Scares Muslin souls – away –
If Broadcloth Hearts are firmer –
Than those of Organdy –

[41]

Who is to blame? The Weaver?
Ah, the bewildering thread!
The Tapestries of Paradise
So notelessly – are made!

c. 1861   1891

77
(279)

Tie the Strings to my Life, My Lord,
Then, I am ready to go!
Just a look at the Horses –
Rapid! That will do!

Put me in on the firmest side –
So I shall never fall –
For we must ride to the Judgment –
And it's partly, down Hill –

But never I mind the steepest –
And never I mind the Sea –
Held fast in Everlasting Race –
By my own Choice, and Thee –

Goodbye to the Life I used to live –
And the World I used to know –
And kiss the Hills, for me, just once –
Then – I am ready to go!

c. 1861   1896

78
(280)

I felt a Funeral, in my Brain,
And Mourners to and fro

Kept treading – treading – till it seemed
That Sense was breaking through –

And when they all were seated,
A Service, like a Drum –
Kept beating – beating – till I thought
My Mind was going numb –

And then I heard them lift a Box
And creak across my Soul
With those same Boots of Lead, again,
Then Space – began to toll,

As all the Heavens were a Bell,
And Being, but an Ear,
And I, and Silence, some strange Race
Wrecked, solitary, here –

And then a Plank in Reason, broke,
And I dropped down, and down –
And hit a World, at every plunge,
And Finished knowing – then –

c. 1861   *1896*

79
(281)

'Tis so appalling – it exhilarates –
So over Horror, it half Captivates –
The Soul stares after it, secure –
A Sepulchre, fears frost, no more –

To scan a Ghost, is faint –
But grappling, conquers it –
How easy, Torment, now –
Suspense kept sawing so –

[43]

The Truth, is Bald, and Cold –
But that will hold –
If any are not sure –
We show them – prayer –
But we, who know,
Stop hoping, now –

Looking at Death, is Dying –
Just let go the Breath –
And not the pillow at your Cheek
So Slumbereth –

Others, Can wrestle –
Yours, is done –
And so of Woe, bleak dreaded – come,
It sets the Fright at liberty –
And Terror's free –
Gay, Ghastly, Holiday!

c. 1861   *1935*

80
(282)

How noteless Men, and Pleiads, stand,
Until a sudden sky
Reveals the fact that One is rapt
Forever from the Eye –

Members of the Invisible,
Existing, while we stare,
In Leagueless Opportunity,
O'ertakeless, as the Air –

Why didn't we detain Them?
The Heavens with a smile,

Sweep by our disappointed Heads
Without a syllable –

c. 1861   *1929*

81
(284)
The Drop, that wrestles in the Sea –
Forgets her own locality –
As I – toward Thee –

She knows herself an incense small –
Yet *small* – she sighs – if *All* – is *All* –
How *larger* – be?

The Ocean – smiles – at her Conceit –
But *she*, forgetting Amphitrite –
Pleads – "Me"?

c. 1861   *1945*

82
(285)
The Robin's my Criterion for Tune –
Because I grow – where Robins do –
But, were I Cuckoo born –
I'd swear by him –
The ode familiar – rules the Noon –
The Buttercup's, my Whim for Bloom –
Because, we're Orchard sprung –
But, were I Britain born,
I'd Daisies spurn –

[45]

None but the Nut – October fit –
Because, through dropping it,
The Seasons flit – I'm taught –
Without the Snow's Tableau
Winter, were lie – to me –
Because I see – New Englandly –
The Queen, discerns like me –
Provincially –

c. 1861   1929

83
(286)

That after Horror – that 'twas *us* –
That passed the mouldering Pier –
Just as the Granite Crumb let go –
Our Savior, by a Hair –

A second more, had dropped too deep
For Fisherman to plumb –
The very profile of the Thought
Puts Recollection numb –

The possibility – to pass
Without a Moment's Bell –
Into Conjecture's presence –
Is like a Face of Steel –
That suddenly looks into ours
With a metallic grin –
The Cordiality of Death –
Who drills his Welcome in –

c. 1861   1935

84
(287)

A Clock stopped –
Not the Mantel's –
Geneva's farthest skill
Can't put the puppet bowing –
That just now dangled still –

An awe came on the Trinket!
The Figures hunched, with pain –
Then quivered out of Decimals –
Into Degreeless Noon –

It will not stir for Doctors –
This Pendulum of snow –
This Shopman importunes it –
While cool – concernless No –

Nods from the Gilded pointers –
Nods from the Seconds slim –
Decades of Arrogance between
The Dial life –
And Him –

c. 1861   *1896*

85
(288)

I'm Nobody! Who are you?
Are you – Nobody – Too?
Then there's a pair of us?
Don't tell! they'd advertise – you know!

How dreary – to be – Somebody!
How public – like a Frog –

[47]

To tell one's name – the livelong June –
To an admiring Bog!

c. *1861*   *1891*

86
(289)

I know some lonely Houses off the Road
A Robber'd like the look of –
Wooden barred,
And Windows hanging low,
Inviting to –
A Portico,
Where two could creep –
One – hand the Tools –
The other peep –
To make sure All's Asleep –
Old fashioned eyes –
Not easy to surprise!

How orderly the Kitchen'd look, by night,
With just a Clock –
But they could gag the Tick –
And Mice won't bark –
And so the Walls – don't tell –
None – will –

A pair of Spectacles ajar just stir –
An Almanac's aware –
Was it the Mat – winked,
Or a Nervous Star?
The Moon – slides down the stair,
To see who's there!

There's plunder – where –
Tankard, or Spoon –

[48]

Earring – or Stone –
A Watch – Some Ancient Brooch
To match the Grandmama –
Staid sleeping – there –

Day – rattles – too
Stealth's – slow –
The Sun has got as far
As the third Sycamore –
Screams Chanticleer
"Who's there"?

And Echoes – Trains away,
Sneer – "Where"!
While the old Couple, just astir,
Fancy the Sunrise – left the door ajar!

c. 1861   *1890*

87
(290)

Of Bronze – and Blaze –
The North – Tonight –
So adequate – it forms –
So preconcerted with itself –
So distant – to alarms –
An Unconcern so sovereign
To Universe, or me –
Infects my simple spirit
With Taints of Majesty –
Till I take vaster attitudes –
And strut upon my stem –
Disdaining Men, and Oxygen,
For Arrogance of them –

[49]

My Splendors, are Menagerie –
But their Competeless Show
Will entertain the Centuries
When I, am long ago,
An Island in dishonored Grass –
Whom none but Beetles – know.

c. 1861   *1896*

88
(292)

If your Nerve, deny you –
Go above your Nerve –
He can lean against the Grave,
If he fear to swerve –

That's a steady posture –
Never any bend
Held of those Brass arms –
Best Giant made –

If your Soul seesaw –
Lift the Flesh door –
The Poltroon wants Oxygen –
Nothing more –

c. 1861   *1935*

89
(293)

I got so I could take his name –
Without – Tremendous gain –

[50]

That Stop-sensation – on my Soul –
And Thunder – in the Room –

I got so I could walk across
That Angle in the floor,
Where he turned so, and I turned – how –
And all our Sinew tore –

I got so I could stir the Box –
In which his letters grew
Without that forcing, in my breath –
As Staples – driven through –

Could dimly recollect a Grace –
I think, they call it "God" –
Renowned to ease Extremity –
When Formula, had failed –

And shape my Hands –
Petition's way,
Tho' ignorant of a word
That Ordination – utters –

My Business, with the Cloud,
If any Power behind it, be,
Not subject to Despair –
It care, in some remoter way,
For so minute affair
As Misery –
Itself, too vast, for interrupting – more –

c 1861   1929

90
(294)
The Doomed – regard the Sunrise
With different Delight –

[51]

Because – when next it burns abroad
They doubt to witness it –

The Man – to die – tomorrow –
Harks for the Meadow Bird –
Because its Music stirs the Axe
That clamors for his head –

Joyful – to whom the Sunrise
Precedes Enamored – Day –
Joyful – for whom the Meadow Bird
Has ought but Elegy!

c. 1861   1929

91
(298)

Alone, I cannot be –
For Hosts – do visit me –
Recordless Company –
Who baffle Key –

They have no Robes, nor Names –
No Almanacs – nor Climes –
But general Homes
Like Gnomes –

Their Coming, may be known
By Couriers within –
Their going – is not –
For they're never gone –

c. 1861   1932

Your Riches – taught me – Poverty.
Myself – a Millionaire
In little Wealths, as Girls could boast
Till broad as Buenos Ayre –

You drifted your Dominions –
A Different Peru –
And I esteemed All Poverty
For Life's Estate with you –

Of Mines, I little know – myself –
But just the names, of Gems –
The Colors of the Commonest –
And scarce of Diadems –

So much, that did I meet the Queen –
Her Glory I should know –
But this, must be a different Wealth –
To miss it – beggars so –

I'm sure 'tis India – all Day –
To those who look on You –
Without a stint – without a blame,
Might I – but be the Jew –

I'm sure it is Golconda –
Beyond my power to deem –
To have a smile for Mine – each Day,
How better, than a Gem!

At least, it solaces to know
That there exists – a Gold –
Altho' I prove it, just in time
Its distance – to behold –

Its far – far Treasure to surmise –
And estimate the Pearl –

[53]

That slipped my simple fingers through –
While just a Girl at School.

1862   1891

93
(301)
I reason, Earth is short –
And Anguish – absolute –
And many hurt,
But, what of that?

I reason, we could die –
The best Vitality
Cannot excel Decay,
But, what of that?

I reason, that in Heaven –
Somehow, it will be even –
Some new Equation, given –
But, what of that?

c. 1862   1890

94
(302)
Like Some Old fashioned Miracle
When Summertime is done –
Seems Summer's Recollection
And the Affairs of June

As infinite Tradition
As Cinderella's Bays –

[54]

Or Little John – of Lincoln Green –
Or Blue Beard's Galleries –

Her Bees have a fictitious Hum –
Her Blossoms, like a Dream –
Elate us – till we almost weep –
So plausible – they seem –

Her Memories like Strains – Review –
When Orchestra is dumb –
The Violin in Baize replaced –
And Ear – and Heaven – numb –

c. 1862   *1914*

95
(303)

The Soul selects her own Society –
Then – shuts the Door –
To her divine Majority –
Present no more –

Unmoved – she notes the Chariots – pausing –
At her low Gate –
Unmoved – an Emperor be kneeling
Upon her Mat –

I've known her – from an ample nation –
Choose One –
Then – close the Valves of her attention –
Like Stone –

c. 1862   *1890*

The Day came slow – till Five o'clock –
Then sprang before the Hills
Like Hindered Rubies – or the Light
A Sudden Musket – spills –

The Purple could not keep the East –
The Sunrise shook abroad
Like Breadths of Topaz – packed a Night –
The Lady just unrolled –

The Happy Winds – their Timbrels took –
The Birds – in docile Rows
Arranged themselves around their Prince
The Wind – is Prince of Those –

The Orchard sparkled like a Jew –
How mighty 'twas – to be
A Guest in this stupendous place –
The Parlor – of the Day –

c 1862   1891

The difference between Despair
And Fear – is like the One
Between the instant of a Wreck –
And when the Wreck has been –

The Mind is smooth – no Motion –
Contented as the Eye
Upon the Forehead of a Bust –
That knows – it cannot see –

c. 1862   1914

98
(306)
The Soul's Superior instants
Occur to Her – alone –
When friend – and Earth's occasion
Have infinite withdrawn –

Or She – Herself – ascended
To too remote a Height
For lower Recognition
Than Her Omnipotent –

This Mortal Abolition
Is seldom – but as fair
As Apparition – subject
To Autocratic Air –

Eternity's disclosure
To favorites – a few –
Of the Colossal substance
Of Immortality

c. 1862

1914

99
(307)
The One who could repeat the Summer day –
Were greater than itself – though He
Minutest of Mankind should be –

And He – could reproduce the Sun –
At period of going down –
The Lingering – and the Stain – I mean –

When Orient have been outgrown –
And Occident – become Unknown –
His Name – remain –

c. 1862   *1891*

100
(308)
I send Two Sunsets –
Day and I – in competition ran –
I finished Two – and several Stars –
While He – was making One –

His own was ampler – but as I
Was saying to a friend –
Mine – is the more convenient
To Carry in the Hand –

c. 1862   *1914*

101
(310)
Give little Anguish –
Lives will fret –
Give Avalanches –
And they'll slant –
Straighten – look cautious for their Breath –
But make no syllable – like Death –
Who only shows his Marble Disc –
Sublimer sort – than Speech –

c. 1862   *1924*

It sifts from Leaden Sieves –
It powders all the Wood.
It fills with Alabaster Wool
The Wrinkles of the Road –

It makes an Even Face
Of Mountain, and of Plain –
Unbroken Forehead from the East
Unto the East again –

It reaches to the Fence –
It wraps it Rail by Rail
Till it is lost in Fleeces –
It deals Celestial Vail

To Stump, and Stack – and Stem –
A Summer's empty Room –
Acres of Joints, where Harvests were,
Recordless, but for them –

It Ruffles Wrists of Posts
As Ankles of a Queen –
Then stills its Artisans – like Ghosts –
Denying they have been –

c. 1862   1891

103
(313)
I should have been too glad, I see --
Too lifted – for the scant degree
Of Life's penurious Round –

[59]

My little Circuit would have shamed
This new Circumference – have blamed –
The homelier time behind.

I should have been too saved – I see –
Too rescued – Fear too dim to me
That I could spell the Prayer
I knew so perfect – yesterday –
That Scalding One – Sabachthani –
Recited fluent – here –

Earth would have been too much – I see –
And Heaven – not enough for me –
I should have had the Joy
Without the Fear – to justify –
The Palm – without the Calvary –
So Savior – Crucify –

Defeat – whets Victory – they say –
The Reefs – in old Gethsemane –
Endear the Coast – beyond!
'Tis Beggars – Banquets – can define –
'Tis Parching – vitalizes Wine –
"Faith" bleats – to understand!

c. 1862   1891

104
(314)
Nature – sometimes sears a Sapling –
Sometimes – scalps a Tree –
Her Green People recollect it
When they do not die –

Fainter Leaves – to Further Seasons –
Dumbly testify –

[60]

We – who have the Souls –
Die oftener – Not so vitally –

c. 1862   1945

105
(315)

He fumbles at your Soul
As Players at the Keys
Before they drop full Music on –
He stuns you by degrees –
Prepares your brittle Nature
For the Ethereal Blow
By fainter Hammers – further heard –
Then nearer – Then so slow
Your Breath has time to straighten –
Your Brain – to bubble Cool –
Deals – One – imperial – Thunderbolt –
That scalps your naked Soul –

When Winds take Forests in their Paws –
The Universe – is still –

c. 1862   1896

106
(318)

I'll tell you how the Sun rose –
A Ribbon at a time –
The Steeples swam in Amethyst –
The news, like Squirrels, ran –

The Hills untied their Bonnets –
The Bobolinks – begun –
Then I said softly to myself –
"That must have been the Sun"!
But how he set – I know not –
There seemed a purple stile
That little Yellow boys and girls
Were climbing all the while –
Till when they reached the other side,
A Dominie in Gray –
Put gently up the evening Bars –
And led the flock away –

c. 1860   1890

107
(319)

The nearest Dream recedes – unrealized –
The Heaven we chase,
Like the June Bee – before the School Boy,
Invites the Race –
Stoops – to an easy Clover –
Dips – evades – teases – deploys –
Then – to the Royal Clouds
Lifts his light Pinnace –
Heedless of the Boy –
Staring – bewildered – at the mocking sky –

Homesick for steadfast Honey –
Ah, the Bee flies not
That brews that rare variety!

c. 1861   1891

108
(320)

We play at Paste –
Till qualified, for Pearl –
Then, drop the Paste –
And deem ourself a fool –

The Shapes – though – were similar –
And our new Hands
Learned *Gem*-Tactics –
Practicing *Sands* –

c. 1862   *1891*

109
(321)

Of all the Sounds despatched abroad,
There's not a Charge to me
Like that old measure in the Boughs –
That phraseless Melody –
The Wind does – working like a Hand,
Whose fingers Comb the Sky –
Then quiver down – with tufts of Tune –
Permitted Gods, and me –

Inheritance, it is, to us –
Beyond the Art to Earn –
Beyond the trait to take away
By Robber, since the Gain
Is gotten not of fingers –
And inner than the Bone –
Hid golden, for the whole of Days,
And even in the Urn,

[63]

I cannot vouch the merry Dust
Do not arise and play
In some odd fashion of its own,
Some quainter Holiday,
When Winds go round and round in Bands –
And thrum upon the door,
And Birds take places, overhead,
To bear them Orchestra.

I crave Him grace of Summer Boughs,
If such an Outcast be –
Who never heard that fleshless Chant –
Rise – solemn – on the Tree,
As if some Caravan of Sound
Off Deserts, in the Sky,
Had parted Rank,
Then knit, and swept –
In Seamless Company –

c. 1862   1890

110
(322)

There came a Day at Summer's full,
Entirely for me –
I thought that such were for the Saints,
Where Resurrections – be –

The Sun, as common, went abroad,
The flowers, accustomed, blew,
As if no soul the solstice passed
That maketh all things new –

The time was scarce profaned, by speech –
The symbol of a word

Was needless, as at Sacrament,
The Wardrobe – of our Lord –

Each was to each The Sealed Church,
Permitted to commune this – time –
Lest we too awkward show
At Supper of the Lamb.

The Hours slid fast – as Hours will,
Clutched tight, by greedy hands –
So faces on two Decks, look back,
Bound to opposing lands –

And so when all the time had leaked,
Without external sound
Each bound the Other's Crucifix –
We gave no other Bond –

Sufficient troth, that we shall rise –
Deposed – at length, the Grave –
To that new Marriage,
Justified – through Calvaries of Love –

c. 1861   *1890*

III
(323)
As if I asked a common Alms,
And in my wondering hand
A Stranger pressed a Kingdom,
And I, bewildered, stand –
As if I asked the Orient
Had it for me a Morn –

[65]

And it should lift its purple Dikes,
And shatter me with Dawn!

c. *1858*

1891

112
(324)
Some keep the Sabbath going to Church –
I keep it, staying at Home –
With a Bobolink for a Chorister –
And an Orchard, for a Dome –

Some keep the Sabbath in Surplice –
I just wear my Wings –
And instead of tolling the Bell, for Church,
Our little Sexton – sings.

God preaches, a noted Clergyman –
And the sermon is never long,
So instead of getting to Heaven, at last –
I'm going, all along.

c. *1860*

1864

113
(325)
Of Tribulation, these are They,
Denoted by the White –
The Spangled Gowns, a lesser Rank
Of Victors – designate –

All these – did conquer –
But the ones who overcame most times –

Wear nothing commoner than Snow –
No Ornament, but Palms –

Surrender – is a sort unknown –
On this superior soil –
Defeat – an outgrown Anguish –
Remembered, as the Mile

Our panting Ankle barely passed –
When Night devoured the Road –
But we – stood whispering in the House –
And all we said – was "Saved"!

c. 1861   *1891*

114
(326)
I cannot dance upon my Toes –
No Man instructed me –
But oftentimes, among my mind,
A Glee possesseth me,

That had I Ballet knowledge –
Would put itself abroad
In Pirouette to blanch a Troupe –
Or lay a Prima, mad,

And though I had no Gown of Gauze –
No Ringlet, to my Hair,
Nor hopped to Audiences – like Birds,
One Claw upon the Air,

Nor tossed my shape in Eider Balls,
Nor rolled on wheels of snow
Till I was out of sight, in sound,
The House encore me so –

[67]

Nor any know I know the Art
I mention – easy – Here –
Nor any Placard boast me –
It's full as Opera –

c. *1862*

1929

115
(327)

Before I got my eye put out
I liked as well to see –
As other Creatures, that have Eyes
And know no other way –

But were it told to me – Today –
That I might have the sky
For mine – I tell you that my Heart
Would split, for size of me –

The Meadows – mine –
The Mountains – mine –
All Forests – Stintless Stars –
As much of Noon as I could take
Between my finite eyes –

The Motions of the Dipping Birds –
The Morning's Amber Road –
For mine – to look at when I liked –
The News would strike me dead –

So safer – guess – with just my soul
Upon the Window pane –
Where other Creatures put their eyes –
Incautious – of the Sun –

c. *1862*

1891

116
(328)

A Bird came down the Walk –
He did not know I saw –
He bit an Angleworm in halves
And ate the fellow, raw,

And then he drank a Dew
From a convenient Grass –
And then hopped sidewise to the Wall
To let a Beetle pass –

He glanced with rapid eyes
That hurried all around –
They looked like frightened Beads, I thought –
He stirred his Velvet Head

Like one in danger, Cautious,
I offered him a Crumb
And he unrolled his feathers
And rowed him softer home –

Than Oars divide the Ocean,
Too silver for a seam –
Or Butterflies, off Banks of Noon
Leap, plashless as they swim.

c. 1862

1891

117
(332)

There are two Ripenings – one – of sight –
Whose forces Spheric wind
Until the Velvet product
Drop spicy to the ground –

[69]

A homelier maturing –
A process in the Bur –
That teeth of Frosts alone disclose
In far October Air.

c. 1862   *1894*

118
(333)

The Grass so little has to do –
A Sphere of simple Green –
With only Butterflies to brood
And Bees to entertain –

And stir all day to pretty Tunes
The Breezes fetch along –
And hold the Sunshine in its lap
And bow to everything –

And thread the Dews, all night, like Pearls –
And make itself so fine
A Duchess were too common
For such a noticing –

And even when it dies – to pass
In Odors so divine –
Like Lowly spices, lain to sleep –
Or Spikenards, perishing –

And then, in Sovereign Barns to dwell –
And dream the Days away,
The Grass so little has to do
I wish I were a Hay –

c. 1862   *1890*

[70]

'Tis not that Dying hurts us so –
'Tis Living – hurts us more –
But Dying – is a different way –
A Kind behind the Door –

The Southern Custom – of the Bird –
That ere the Frosts are due –
Accepts a better Latitude –
We – are the Birds – that stay.

The Shiverers round Farmers' doors –
For whose reluctant Crumb –
We stipulate – till pitying Snows
Persuade our Feathers Home.

c. 1862   1945

I know that He exists.
Somewhere – in Silence –
He has hid his rare life
From our gross eyes.

'Tis an instant's play.
'Tis a fond Ambush –
Just to make Bliss
Earn her own surprise!

But – should the play
Prove piercing earnest –
Should the glee – glaze –
In Death's – stiff – stare –

Would not the fun
Look too expensive!
Would not the jest –
Have crawled too far!

c. 1862   1891

121
(339)
I tend my flowers for thee –
Bright Absentee!
My Fuchsia's Coral Seams
Rip – while the Sower – dreams –

Geraniums – tint – and spot –
Low Daisies – dot –
My Cactus – splits her Beard
To show her throat –

Carnations – tip their spice –
And Bees – pick up –
A Hyacinth – I hid –
Puts out a Ruffled Head –
And odors fall
From flasks – so small –
You marvel how they held –

Globe Roses – break their satin flake –
Upon my Garden floor –
Yet – thou – not there –
I had as lief they bore
No Crimson – more –

Thy flower – be gay –
Her Lord – away!
It ill becometh me –

I'll dwell in Calyx – Gray –
How modestly – alway –
Thy Daisy –
Draped for thee!

c. 1862   *1929*

122
(341)

After great pain, a formal feeling comes –
The Nerves sit ceremonious, like Tombs –
The stiff Heart questions was it He, that bore,
And Yesterday, or Centuries before?

The Feet, mechanical, go round –
Of Ground, or Air, or Ought –
A Wooden way
Regardless grown,
A Quartz contentment, like a stone –

This is the Hour of Lead –
Remembered, if outlived,
As Freezing persons, recollect the Snow –
First – Chill – then Stupor – then the letting go –

c. 1862   *1929*

123
(342)

It will be Summer – eventually.
Ladies – with parasols –

[73]

Sauntering Gentlemen – with Canes –
And little Girls – with Dolls –

Will tint the pallid landscape –
As 'twere a bright Bouquet –
Tho' drifted deep, in Parian –
The Village lies – today –

The Lilacs – bending many a year –
Will sway with purple load –
The Bees – will not despise the tune –
Their Forefathers – have hummed –

The Wild Rose – redden in the Bog –
The Aster – on the Hill
Her everlasting fashion – set –
And Covenant Gentians – frill –

Till Summer folds her miracle –
As Women – do – their Gown –
Or Priests – adjust the Symbols –
When Sacrament – is done –

?. 1862   1929

124
(345)

Funny – to be a Century –
And see the People – going by –
I – should die of the Oddity –
But then – I'm not so staid – as He –

He keeps His Secrets safely – very –
Were He to tell – extremely sorry
This Bashful Globe of Ours would be –
So dainty of Publicity –

c. 1862   1929

125
(346)

Not probable – The barest Chance –
A smile too few – a word too much
And far from Heaven as the Rest –
The Soul so close on Paradise –

What if the Bird from journey far –
Confused by Sweets – as Mortals – are –
Forget the secret of His wing
And perish – but a Bough between –
Oh, Groping feet –
Oh Phantom Queen!

c. 1862

1935

126
(348)

I dreaded that first Robin, so,
But He is mastered, now,
I'm some accustomed to Him grown,
He hurts a little, though –

I thought if I could only live
Till that first Shout got by –
Not all Pianos in the Woods
Had power to mangle me –

I dared not meet the Daffodils –
For fear their Yellow Gown
Would pierce me with a fashion
So foreign to my own –

I wished the Grass would hurry –
So – when 'twas time to see –

He'd be too tall, the tallest one
Could stretch – to look at me –

I could not bear the Bees should come,
I wished they'd stay away
In those dim countries where they go,
What word had they, for me?

They're here, though; not a creature failed –
No Blossom stayed away
In gentle deference to me –
The Queen of Calvary –

Each one salutes me, as he goes,
And I, my childish Plumes,
Lift, in bereaved acknowledgment
Of their unthinking Drums –

c. 1862   *1891*

127
(350)

They leave us with the Infinite.
But He – is not a man –
His fingers are the size of fists –
His fists, the size of men –

And whom he foundeth, with his Arm
As Himmaleh, shall stand –
Gibraltar's Everlasting Shoe
Poised lightly on his Hand,

So trust him, Comrade –
You for you, and I, for you and me
Eternity is ample,
And quick enough, if true.

c. 1862   *1945*

[76]

128
(351)

I felt my life with both my hands
To see if it was there –
I held my spirit to the Glass,
To prove it possibler –

I turned my Being round and round
And paused at every pound
To ask the Owner's name –
For doubt, that I should know the Sound –

I judged my features – jarred my hair –
I pushed my dimples by, and waited –
If they – twinkled back –
Conviction might, of me –

I told myself, "Take Courage, Friend –
That – was a former time –
But we might learn to like the Heaven,
As well as our Old Home!"

c. 1862   1945

129
(355)

'Tis Opposites – entice –
Deformed Men – ponder Grace –
Bright fires – the Blanketless –
The Lost – Day's face –

The Blind – esteem it be
Enough Estate – to see –
The Captive – strangles new –
For deeming – Beggars – play –

[77]

To lack – enamor Thee –
Tho' the Divinity –
Be only
Me –

c. 1862   1929

130
(357)
God is a distant – stately Lover –
Woos, as He states us – by His Son –
Verily, a Vicarious Courtship –
"Miles", and "Priscilla", were such an One –

But, lest the Soul – like fair "Priscilla"
Choose the Envoy – and spurn the Groom –
Vouches, with hyperbolic archness –
"Miles", and "John Alden" were Synonym –

1862   1891

131
(360)
Death sets a Thing significant
The Eye had hurried by
Except a perished Creature
Entreat us tenderly

To ponder little Workmanships
In Crayon, or in Wool,
With "This was last Her fingers did" –
Industrious until –

[78]

The Thimble weighed too heavy –
The stitches stopped – themselves –
And then 'twas put among the Dust
Upon the Closet shelves –

A Book I have – a friend gave –
Whose Pencil – here and there –
Had notched the place that pleased Him –
At Rest – His fingers are –

Now – when I read – I read not –
For interrupting Tears –
Obliterate the Etchings
Too Costly for Repairs.

c. 1862   1891

132
(364)
The Morning after Woe –
'Tis frequently the Way –
Surpasses all that rose before –
For utter Jubilee –

As Nature did not care –
And piled her Blossoms on –
And further to parade a Joy
Her Victim stared upon –

The Birds declaim their Tunes –
Pronouncing every word
Like Hammers – Did they know they fell
Like Litanies of Lead –

On here and there – a creature –
They'd modify the Glee

[79]

To fit some Crucifixal Clef –
Some Key of Calvary –

c. 1862

1935

133
(365)
Dare you see a Soul *at the White Heat?*
Then crouch within the door –
Red – is the Fire's common tint –
But when the vivid Ore
Has vanquished Flame's conditions,
It quivers from the Forge
Without a color, but the light
Of unanointed Blaze.
Least Village has its Blacksmith
Whose Anvil's even ring
Stands symbol for the finer Forge
That soundless tugs – within –
Refining these impatient Ores
With Hammer, and with Blaze
Until the Designated Light
Repudiate the Forge –

c. 1862

1891

134
(367)
Over and over, like a Tune –
The Recollection plays –
Drums off the Phantom Battlements
Cornets of Paradise –

Snatches, from Baptized Generations –
Cadences too grand
But for the Justified Processions
At the Lord's Right hand.

c. 1862   1929

135
(368)

How sick – to wait – in any place – but thine –
I knew last night – when someone tried to twine –
Thinking – perhaps – that I looked tired – or alone –
Or breaking – almost – with unspoken pain –

And I turned – ducal –
That right – was thine –
One port – suffices – for a Brig – like *mine* –

Ours be the tossing – wild though the sea –
Rather than a Mooring – unshared by thee.
Ours be the Cargo – *unladen – here* –
Rather than the *"spicy isles – "*
And thou – not there –

c. 1862   1945

136
(369)

She lay as if at play
I lei lifc had looped away –
Intending to return –
But not so soon –

[81]

Her merry Arms, half dropt –
As if for lull of sport –
An instant had forgot –
The Trick to start –

Her dancing Eyes – ajar –
As if their Owner were
Still sparkling through
For fun – at you –

Her Morning at the door –
Devising, I am sure –
To force her sleep –
So light – so deep –

c. 1862   1935

137
(370)
Heaven is so far of the Mind
That were the Mind dissolved –
The Site – of it – by Architect
Could not again be proved –

'Tis vast – as our Capacity –
As fair – as our idea –
To Him of adequate desire
No further 'tis, than Here –

c. 1862   1929

138
(373)
I'm saying every day
"If I should be a Queen, tomorrow" –

[82]

I'd do this way –
And so I deck, a little,

If it be, I wake a Bourbon,
None on me, bend supercilious –
With "This was she –
Begged in the Market place –
Yesterday."

Court is a stately place –
I've heard men say –
So I loop my apron, against the Majesty
With bright Pins of Buttercup –
That not too plain –
Rank – overtake me –

And perch my Tongue
On Twigs of singing – rather high –
But this, might be my brief Term
To qualify –

Put from my simple speech all plain word –
Take other accents, as such I heard
Though but for the Cricket – just,
And but for the Bee –
Not in all the Meadow –
One accost me –

Better to be ready –
Than did next morn
Meet me in Aragon –
My old Gown – on –

And the surprised Air
Rustics – wear –
Summoned – unexpectedly –
To Exeter –

c. 1862

1935

139
(374)
I went to Heaven –
'Twas a small Town –
Lit – with a Ruby –
Lathed – with Down –

Stiller – than the fields
At the full Dew –
Beautiful – as Pictures –
No Man drew.
People – like the Moth –
Of Mechlin – frames –
Duties – of Gossamer –
And Eider – names –
Almost – contented –
I – could be –
'Mong such unique
Society –

c. 1862   *1891*

140
(375)
The Angle of a Landscape –
That every time I wake –
Between my Curtain and the Wall
Upon an ample Crack –

Like a Venetian – waiting –
Accosts my open eye –
Is just a Bough of Apples –
Held slanting, in the Sky –

The Pattern of a Chimney –
The Forehead of a Hill –

[84]

Sometimes – a Vane's Forefinger –
But that's – Occasional –

The Seasons – shift – my Picture –
Upon my Emerald Bough,
I wake – to find no – Emeralds –
Then – Diamonds – which the Snow

From Polar Caskets – fetched me –
The Chimney – and the Hill –
And just the Steeple's finger –
These – never stir at all –

c. 1862   1945

141
(376)
Of Course – I prayed –
And did God Care?
He cared as much as on the Air
A Bird – had stamped her foot –
And cried "Give Me" –
My Reason – Life –
I had not had – but for Yourself –
'Twere better Charity
To leave me in the Atom's Tomb –
Merry, and Nought, and gay, and numb –
Than this smart Misery.

c. 1862   1929

142
(378)
I saw no Way – The Heavens were stitched –
I felt the Columns close –

The Earth reversed her Hemispheres –
I touched the Universe –

And back it slid – and I alone –
A Speck upon a Ball –
Went out upon Circumference –
Beyond the Dip of Bell –

c. 1862   *1935*

143
(379)

Rehearsal to Ourselves
Of a Withdrawn Delight –
Affords a Bliss like Murder –
Omnipotent – Acute –

We will not drop the Dirk –
Because We love the Wound
The Dirk Commemorate – Itself
Remind Us that we died.

c. 1862   *1929*

144
(381)

A Secret told –
Ceases to be a Secret – then –
A Secret – kept –
That – can appal but One –

Better of it – continual be afraid –
Than it –
And Whom you told it to – beside –

c. 1862   *1929*

[86]

145
(382)

For Death – or rather
For the Things 'twould buy –
This – put away
Life's Opportunity –

The Things that Death will buy
Are Room –
Escape from Circumstances –
And a Name –

With Gifts of Life
How Death's Gifts may compare –
We know not –
For the Rates – lie Here –

c. 1862   1914

146
(383)

Exhilaration – is within –
There can no Outer Wine
So royally intoxicate
As that diviner Brand

The Soul achieves – Herself –
To drink – or set away
For Visitor – Or Sacrament –
'Tis not of Holiday

To stimulate a Man
Who hath the Ample Rhine
Within his Closet – Best you can
Exhale in offering.

c. 1862   1935

147
(384)

No Rack can torture me –
My Soul – at Liberty –
Behind this mortal Bone
There knits a bolder One –

You cannot prick with saw –
Nor pierce with Scimitar –
Two Bodies – therefore be –
Bind One – The Other fly –

The Eagle of his Nest
No easier divest –
And gain the Sky
Than mayest Thou –

Except Thyself may be
Thine Enemy –
Captivity is Consciousness –
So's Liberty.

c. 1862   *1890*

148
(386)

Answer July –
Where is the Bee –
Where is the Blush –
Where is the Hay?

Ah, said July –
Where is the Seed –
Where is the Bud –
Where is the May –
Answer Thee – Me –

[88]

Nay – said the May –
Show me the Snow –
Show me the Bells –
Show me the Jay!

Quibbled the Jay –
Where be the Maize –
Where be the Haze –
Where be the Bur?
Here – said the Year –

c. 1862   *1935*

149
(389)

There's been a Death, in the Opposite House,
As lately as Today –
I know it, by the numb look
Such Houses have – alway –

The Neighbors rustle in and out –
The Doctor – drives away –
A Window opens like a Pod –
Abrupt – mechanically –

Somebody flings a Mattress out –
The Children hurry by –
They wonder if it died – on that –
I used to – when a Boy –

The Minister – goes stiffly in –
As if the House were His –
And He owned all the Mourners – now –
And little Boys – besides –

And then the Milliner – and the Man
Of the Appalling Trade –
To take the measure of the House –

There'll be that Dark Parade –

Of Tassels – and of Coaches – soon –
It's easy as a Sign –
The Intuition of the News –
In just a Country Town –

c. 1862   1896

150
(391)

A Visitor in Marl –
Who influences Flowers –
Till they are orderly as Busts –
And Elegant – as Glass –

Who visits in the Night –
And just before the Sun –
Concludes his glistening interview –
Caresses – and is gone –

But whom his fingers touched –
And where his feet have run –
And whatsoever Mouth he kissed –
Is as it had not been –

c. 1862   1935

151
(392)

Through the Dark Sod – as Education –
The Lily passes sure –

[90]

Feels her white foot – no trepidation –
Her faith – no fear –

Afterward – in the Meadow –
Swinging her Beryl Bell –
The Mold-life – all forgotten – now –
In Ecstasy – and Dell –

c. 1862   *1929*

152
(396)

There is a Languor of the Life
More imminent than Pain –
'Tis Pain's Successor – When the Soul
Has suffered all it can –

A Drowsiness – diffuses –
A Dimness like a Fog
Envelops Consciousness –
As Mists – obliterate a Crag.

The Surgeon – does not blanch – at pain –
His Habit – is severe –
But tell him that it ceased to feel –
The Creature lying there –

And he will tell you – skill is late –
A Mightier than He –
Has ministered before Him –
There's no Vitality.

c. 1862   *1929*

152-A
(398)
[See page 321 for the poem text.]

153
(399)

A House upon the Height –
That Wagon never reached –
No Dead, were ever carried down –
No Peddler's Cart – approached –

Whose Chimney never smoked –
Whose Windows – Night and Morn –
Caught Sunrise first – and Sunset – last –
Then – held an Empty Pane –

Whose fate – Conjecture knew –
No other neighbor – did –
And what it was – we never lisped –
Because He – never told –

c. 1862   1945

154
(401)

What Soft – Cherubic Creatures –
These Gentlewomen are –
One would as soon assault a Plush –
Or violate a Star –

Such Dimity Convictions –
A Horror so refined
Of freckled Human Nature –
Of Deity – ashamed –

It's such a common – Glory –
A Fisherman's – Degree –
Redemption – Brittle Lady –
Be so – ashamed of Thee –

c. 1862   1896

[92]

155
(403)
The Winters are so short –
I'm hardly justified
In sending all the Birds away –
And moving into Pod –

Myself – for scarcely settled –
The Phoebes have begun –
And then – it's time to strike my Tent –
And open House – again –

It's mostly, interruptions –
My Summer – is despoiled –
Because there was a Winter – once –
And all the Cattle – starved –

And so there was a Deluge –
And swept the World away –
But Ararat's a Legend – now –
And no one credits Noah –

c. 1862   *1935*

156
(406)
Some – Work for Immortality –
The Chiefer part, for Time –
He – Compensates – immediately –
The former – Checks – on Fame –

Slow Gold – but Everlasting –
The Bullion of Today –
Contrasted with the Currency
Of Immortality –

[93]

A Beggar – Here and There –
Is gifted to discern
Beyond the Broker's insight –
One's – Money – One's – the Mine –

c. 1862   *1929*

157
(407)

If What we could – were what we would –
Criterion – be small –
It is the Ultimate of Talk –
The Impotence to Tell –

c. 1862   *1914*

158
(408)

Unit, like Death, for Whom?
True, like the Tomb,
Who tells no secret
Told to Him –
The Grave is strict –
Tickets admit
Just two – the Bearer –
And the Borne –
And seat – just One –
The Living – tell –
The Dying – but a Syllable –
The Coy Dead – None –

[94]

No Chatter – here – no tea –
So Babbler, and Bohea – stay there –
But Gravity – and Expectation – and Fear –
A tremor just, that All's not sure.

c. 1862   1947

159
(409)

They dropped like Flakes –
They dropped like Stars –
Like Petals from a Rose –
When suddenly across the June
A wind with fingers – goes –

They perished in the Seamless Grass –
No eye could find the place –
But God can summon every face
On his Repealless – List.

c. 1862   1891

160
(411)

The Color of the Grave is Green –
The Outer Grave – I mean –
You would not know it from the Field –
Except it own a Stone –

To help the fond – to find it –
Too infinite asleep
To stop and tell them where it is –
But just a Daisy – deep –

[95]

The Color of the Grave is white –
The outer Grave – I mean –
You would not know it from the Drifts –
In Winter – till the Sun –

Has furrowed out the Aisles –
Then – higher than the Land
The little Dwelling Houses rise
Where each – has left a friend –

The Color of the Grave within –
The Duplicate – I mean –
Not all the Snows could make it white –
Not all the Summers – Green –

You've seen the Color – maybe –
Upon a Bonnet bound –
When that you met it with before –
The Ferret – cannot find –

c. 1862   1935

161
(412)

I read my sentence – steadily –
Reviewed it with my eyes,
To see that I made no mistake
In its extremest clause –
The Date, and manner, of the shame –
And then the Pious Form
That "God have mercy" on the Soul
The Jury voted Him –
I made my soul familiar – with her extremity –
That at the last, it should not be a novel Agony –

[96]

But she, and Death, acquainted –
Meet tranquilly, as friends –
Salute, and pass, without a Hint –
And there, the Matter ends –

c. *1862*   *1891*

162
(413)

I never felt at Home – Below –
And in the Handsome Skies
I shall not feel at Home – I know –
I don't like Paradise –

Because it's Sunday – all the time –
And Recess – never comes –
And Eden'll be so lonesome
Bright Wednesday Afternoons –

If God could make a visit –
Or ever took a Nap –
So not to see us – but they say
Himself – a Telescope

Perennial beholds us –
Myself would run away
From Him – and Holy Ghost – and All –
But there's the "Judgment Day"!

c. *1862*   *1929*

163
(414)

'Twas like a Maelstrom, with a notch.
That nearer, every Day,

[97]

Kept narrowing its boiling Wheel
Until the Agony

Toyed coolly with the final inch
Of your delirious Hem –
And you dropt, lost,
When something broke –
And let you from a Dream –

As if a Goblin with a Gauge –
Kept measuring the Hours –
Until you felt your Second
Weigh, helpless, in his Paws –

And not a Sinew – stirred – could help,
And sense was setting numb –
When God – remembered – and the Fiend
Let go, then, Overcome –

As if your Sentence stood – pronounced –
And you were frozen led
From Dungeon's luxury of Doubt
To Gibbets, and the Dead –

And when the Film had stitched your eyes
A Creature gasped "Reprieve"!
Which Anguish was the utterest – then –
To perish, or to live?

c. 1862   *1945*

164
(419)
We grow accustomed to the Dark –
When Light is put away –

[98]

As when the Neighbor holds the Lamp
To witness her Goodbye –

A Moment – We uncertain step
For newness of the night –
Then – fit our Vision to the Dark –
And meet the Road – erect –

And so of larger – Darknesses –
Those Evenings of the Brain –
When not a Moon disclose a sign –
Or Star – come out – within –

The Bravest – grope a little –
And sometimes hit a Tree
Directly in the Forehead –
But as they learn to see –

Either the Darkness alters –
Or something in the sight
Adjusts itself to Midnight –
And Life steps almost straight.

c. 1862   1935

165
(423)

The Months have ends – the Years – a knot –
No Power can untie
To stretch a little further
A Skein of Misery –

The Earth lays back these tired lives
In her mysterious Drawers –
Too tenderly, that any doubt
An ultimate Repose –

[99]

The manner of the Children –
Who weary of the Day –
Themself – the noisy Plaything
They cannot put away –

c. 1862 *1935*

166
(424)

Removed from Accident of Loss
By Accident of Gain
Befalling not my simple Days –
Myself had just to earn –

Of Riches – as unconscious
As is the Brown Malay
Of Pearls in Eastern Waters,
Marked His – What Holiday

Would stir his slow conception –
Had he the power to dream
That but the Dower's fraction –
Awaited even – Him –

c. 1862 *1935*

167
(428)

Taking up the fair Ideal,
Just to cast her down
When a fracture – we discover –
Or a splintered Crown –

Makes the Heavens portable –
And the Gods – a lie –
Doubtless – "Adam" – scowled at Eden –
For *his* perjury!

Cherishing – our poor Ideal –
Till in purer dress –
We behold her – glorified –
Comforts – search – like this –
Till the broken creatures –
We adored – for whole –
Stains – all washed –
Transfigured – mended –
Meet us – with a smile –

c. 1862   *1945*

168
(435)
Much Madness is divinest Sense –
To a discerning Eye –
Much Sense – the starkest Madness –
'Tis the Majority
In this, as All, prevail –
Assent – and you are sane –
Demur – you're straightway dangerous –
And handled with a Chain –

c. 1862   *1890*

169
(437)
Prayer is the little implement
Through which Men reach

[101]

Where Presence – is denied them.
They fling their Speech

By means of it – in God's Ear –
If then He hear –
This sums the Apparatus
Comprised in Prayer –

c. 1862   1891

170
(438)
Forget! The lady with the Amulet
Forget she wore it at her Heart
Because she breathed against
Was Treason twixt?

Deny! Did Rose her Bee –
For Privilege of Play
Or Wile of Butterfly
Or Opportunity – Her Lord away?

The lady with the Amulet – will fade –
The Bee – in Mausoleum laid –
Discard his Bride –
But longer than the little Rill –
That cooled the Forehead of the Hill –
While Other – went the Sea to fill –
And Other – went to turn the Mill –
I'll do thy Will –

∴ 1862   1935

171
(439)

Undue Significance a starving man attaches
To Food –
Far off – He sighs – and therefore – Hopeless –
And therefore – Good –

Partaken – it relieves – indeed –
But proves us
That Spices fly
In the Receipt – It was the Distance –
Was Savory –

c. 1862   1891

172
(441)

This is my letter to the World
That never wrote to Me –
The simple News that Nature told –
With tender Majesty

Her Message is committed
To Hands I cannot see –
For love of Her – Sweet – countrymen –
Judge tenderly – of Me

c. 1862   1890

173
(442)

God made a little Gentian –
It tried – to be a Rose –

And failed – and all the Summer laughed –
But just before the Snows

There rose a Purple Creature –
That ravished all the Hill –
And Summer hid her Forehead –
And Mockery – was still –

The Frosts were her condition –
The Tyrian would not come
Until the North – invoke it –
Creator – Shall I – bloom?

c. 1862

1891

174
(443)
I tie my Hat – I crease my Shawl –
Life's little duties do – precisely –
As the very least
Were infinite – to me –

I put new Blossoms in the Glass –
And throw the old – away –
I push a petal from my Gown
That anchored there – I weigh
The time 'twill be till six o'clock
I have so much to do –
And yet – Existence – some way back –
Stopped – struck – my ticking – through –
We cannot put Ourself away
As a completed Man

Or Woman – When the Errand's done
We came to Flesh – upon –
There may be – Miles on Miles of Nought –
Of Action – sicker far –
To simulate – is stinging work –
To cover what we are
From Science – and from Surgery –
Too Telescopic Eyes
To bear on us unshaded –
For their – sake – not for Ours –
'Twould start them –
We – could tremble –
But since we got a Bomb –
And held it in our Bosom –
Nay – Hold it – it is calm –

Therefore – we do life's labor –
Though life's Reward – be done –
With scrupulous exactness –
To hold our Senses – on –

c. 1862   *1929*

175
(445)
'Twas just this time, last year, I died.
I know I heard the Corn,
When I was carried by the Farms –
It had the Tassels on –

I thought how yellow it would look –
When Richard went to mill –

[105]

And then, I wanted to get out,
But something held my will.

I thought just how Red – Apples wedged
The Stubble's joints between –
And the Carts stooping round the fields
To take the Pumpkins in –

I wondered which would miss me, least,
And when Thanksgiving, came,
If Father'd multiply the plates –
To make an even Sum –

And would it blur the Christmas glee
My Stocking hang too high
For any Santa Claus to reach
The Altitude of me –

But this sort, grieved myself,
And so, I thought the other way,
How just this time, some perfect year –
Themself, should come to me –

c. 1862   *1896*

176
(448)
This was a Poet – It is That
Distills amazing sense
From ordinary Meanings –
And Attar so immense

From the familiar species
That perished by the Door –

We wonder it was not Ourselves
Arrested it – before –

Of Pictures, the Discloser –
The Poet – it is He –
Entitles Us – by Contrast –
To ceaseless Poverty –

Of Portion – so unconscious –
The Robbing – could not harm –
Himself – to Him – a Fortune –
Exterior – to Time –

c. 1862   1929

177
(449)

I died for Beauty – but was scarce
Adjusted in the Tomb
When One who died for Truth, was lain
In an adjoining Room –

He questioned softly "Why I failed"?
"For Beauty", I replied –
"And I – for Truth – Themself are One –
We Brethren, are", He said –

And so, as Kinsmen, met a Night –
We talked between the Rooms –
Until the Moss had reached our lips –
And covered up – our names –

c. 1862   1890

178
(452)

The Malay – took the Pearl –
Not – I – the Earl –
I – feared the Sea – too much
Unsanctified – to touch –

Praying that I might be
Worthy – the Destiny –
The Swarthy fellow swam –
And bore my Jewel – Home –

Home to the Hut! What lot
Had I – the Jewel – got –
Borne on a Dusky Breast –
I had not deemed a Vest
Of Amber – fit –

The Negro never knew
I – wooed it – too –
To gain, or be undone –
Alike to Him – One –

c. 1862   *1945*

179
(453)

Love – thou art high –
I cannot climb thee –
But, were it Two –
Who knows but we –
Taking turns – at the Chimborazo –
Ducal – at last – stand up by thee –

[108]

Love thou art deep –
I cannot cross thee –
But, were there Two
Instead of One –
Rower, and Yacht – some sovereign Summer –
Who knows – but we'd reach the Sun?

Love – thou art Veiled –
A few – behold thee –
Smile – and alter – and prattle – and die –
Bliss – were an Oddity – without thee –
Nicknamed by God –
Eternity –

c. 1862   *1929*

180
(455)

Triumph – may be of several kinds –
There's Triumph in the Room
When that Old Imperator – Death –
By Faith – be overcome –

There's Triumph of the finer Mind
When Truth – affronted long –
Advance unmoved – to Her Supreme –
Her God – Her only Throng –

A Triumph – when Temptation's Bribe
Be slowly handed back –
One eye upon the Heaven renounced –
And One – upon the Rack –

Severer Triumph – by Himself
Experienced – who pass

Acquitted – from that Naked Bar –
Jehovah's Countenance –

c. 1862

1891

181
(459)
A Tooth upon Our Peace
The Peace cannot deface –
Then Wherefore be the Tooth?
To vitalize the Grace –

The Heaven hath a Hell –
Itself to signalize –
And every sign before the Place
Is Gilt with Sacrifice –

c. 1862

1935

182
(461)
A Wife – at Daybreak I shall be –
Sunrise – Hast thou a Flag for me?
At Midnight, I am but a Maid,
How short it takes to make a Bride –
Then – Midnight, I have passed from thee
Unto the East, and Victory –

Midnight – Good Night! I hear them call,
The Angels bustle in the Hall –
Softly my Future climbs the Stair,
I fumble at my Childhood's prayer

So soon to be a Child no more –
Eternity, I'm coming – Sir,
Savior – I've seen the face – before!

c. 1862   1929

183
(463)
I live with Him – I see His face –
I go no more away
For Visitor – or Sundown –
Death's single privacy

The Only One – forestalling Mine –
And that – by Right that He
Presents a Claim invisible –
No wedlock – granted Me –

I live with Him – I hear His Voice –
I stand alive – Today –
To witness to the Certainty
Of Immortality –

Taught Me – by Time – the lower Way –
Conviction – Every day –
That Life like This – is stopless –
Be Judgment – what it may –

c. 1862   1896

184
(465)
I heard a Fly buzz – when I died –
The Stillness in the Room

[111]

Was like the Stillness in the Air –
Between the Heaves of Storm –

The Eyes around – had wrung them dry –
And Breaths were gathering firm
For that last Onset – when the King
Be witnessed – in the Room –

I willed my Keepsakes – Signed away
What portion of me be
Assignable – and then it was
There interposed a Fly –

With Blue – uncertain stumbling Buzz –
Between the light – and me –
And then the Windows failed – and then
I could not see to see –

c. 1862   1896

185
(466)

'Tis little I – could care for Pearls –
Who own the ample sea –
Or Brooches – when the Emperor –
With Rubies – pelteth me –

Or Gold – who am the Prince of Mines –
Or Diamonds – when have I
A Diadem to fit a Dome –
Continual upon me –

c. 1862   1896

I am alive – I guess –
The Branches on my Hand
Are full of Morning Glory –
And at my finger's end –

The Carmine – tingles warm –
And if I hold a Glass
Across my Mouth – it blurs it –
Physician's – proof of Breath –

I am alive – because
I am not in a Room –
The Parlor – Commonly – it is –
So Visitors may come –

And lean – and view it sidewise –
And add "How cold – it grew" –
And "Was it conscious – when it stepped
In Immortality?"

I am alive – because
I do not own a House –
Entitled to myself – precise –
And fitting no one else –

And marked my Girlhood's name –
So Visitors may know
Which Door is mine – and not mistake –
And try another Key –

How good – to be alive!
How infinite – to be
Alive – two-fold – The Birth I had –
And this – besides, in – Thee!

c. 1862   1945

187
(472)

Except the Heaven had come so near –
So seemed to choose My Door –
The Distance would not haunt me so –
I had not hoped – before –

But just to hear the Grace depart –
I never thought to see –
Afflicts me with a Double loss –
'Tis lost – And lost to me –

c. 1862   1891

188
(474)

They put Us far apart –
As separate as Sea
And Her unsown Peninsula –
We signified "These see" –

They took away our Eyes –
They thwarted Us with Guns –
"I see Thee" each responded straight
Through Telegraphic Signs –

With Dungeons – They devised –
But through their thickest skill –
And their opaquest Adamant –
Our Souls saw – just as well –

They summoned Us to die –
With sweet alacrity
We stood upon our stapled feet –
Condemned – but just – to see –

[114]

Permission to recant –
Permission to forget –
We turned our backs upon the Sun
For perjury of that –

Not Either – noticed Death –
Of Paradise – aware –
Each other's Face – was all the Disc
Each other's setting – saw –

c. 1862   1935

189
(475)
Doom is the House without the Door –
'Tis entered from the Sun –
And then the Ladder's thrown away,
Because Escape – is done –

'Tis varied by the Dream
Of what they do outside –
Where Squirrels play – and Berries die –
And Hemlocks – bow – to God –

c. 1862   1929

190
(477)
No Man can compass a Despair –
As round a Goalless Road
No faster than a Mile at once
The Traveller proceed –

[115]

Unconscious of the Width –
Unconscious that the Sun
Be setting on His progress –
So accurate the One

At estimating Pain –
Whose own – has just begun ·
His ignorance – the Angel
That pilot Him along –

c 18621935

191
(478)
I had no time to Hate –
Because
The Grave would hinder Me –
And Life was not so
Ample I
Could finish – Enmity –

Nor had I time to Love –
But since
Some Industry must be –
The little Toil of Love –
I thought
Be large enough for Me –

c. 18621890

192
(479)
She dealt her pretty words like Blades –
How glittering they shone –

And every One unbared a Nerve
Or wantoned with a Bone –

She never deemed – she hurt –
That – is not Steel's Affair –
A vulgar grimace in the Flesh –
How ill the Creatures bear –

To Ache is human – not polite –
The Film upon the eye
Mortality's old Custom –
Just locking up – to Die.

c. 1862   1929

193
(480)
"Why do I love" You, Sir?
Because –
The Wind does not require the Grass
To answer – Wherefore when He pass
She cannot keep Her place.

Because He knows – and
Do not You –
And We know not –
Enough for Us
The Wisdom it be so –

The Lightning – never asked an Eye
Wherefore it shut – when He was by –
Because He knows it cannot speak –
And reasons not contained –
– Of Talk –
There be – preferred by Daintier Folk –

The Sunrise – Sir – compelleth Me –
Because He's Sunrise – and I see –
Therefore – Then –
I love Thee –

c. 1862   *1929*

194
(486)

I was the slightest in the House –
I took the smallest Room –
At night, my little Lamp, and Book –
And one Geranium –

So stationed I could catch the Mint
That never ceased to fall –
And just my Basket –
Let me think – I'm sure
That this was all –

I never spoke – unless addressed –
And then, 'twas brief and low –
I could not bear to live – aloud –
The Racket shamed me so –

And if it had not been so far –
And any one I knew
Were going – I had often thought
How noteless – I could die –

c. 1862   *1945*

195
(488)
Myself was formed – a Carpenter –
An unpretending time
My Plane – and I, together wrought
Before a Builder came –

To measure our attainments –
Had we the Art of Boards
Sufficiently developed – He'd hire us
At Halves –

My Tools took Human – Faces –
The Bench, where we had toiled –
Against the Man – persuaded –
We – Temples build – I said –

c. 1862   *1935*

196
(490)
To One denied to drink
To tell what Water is
Would be acuter, would it not
Than letting Him surmise?

To lead Him to the Well
And let Him hear it drip
Remind Him, would it not, somewhat
Of His condemned lip?

c. 1862   *1945*

197
(491)

While it is alive
Until Death touches it
While it and I lap one Air
Dwell in one Blood
Under one Sacrament
Show me Division can split or pare –

Love is like Life – merely longer
Love is like Death, during the Grave
Love is the Fellow of the Resurrection
Scooping up the Dust and chanting "Live"!

c. 1862   *1945*

198
(492)

Civilization – spurns – the Leopard!
Was the Leopard – bold?
Deserts – never rebuked her Satin –
Ethiop – her Gold –
Tawny – her Customs –
She was Conscious –
Spotted – her Dun Gown –
This was the Leopard's nature – Signor –
Need – a keeper – frown?

Pity – the Pard – that left her Asia –
Memories – of Palm –
Cannot be stifled – with Narcotic –
Nor suppressed – with Balm –

c. 1862   *1945*

Going to Him! Happy letter!
Tell Him –
Tell Him the page I didn't write –
Tell Him – I only said the Syntax –
And left the Verb and the pronoun out –
Tell Him just how the fingers hurried –
Then – how they waded – slow – slow –
And then you wished you had eyes in your pages –
So you could see what moved them so –

Tell Him – it wasn't a Practised Writer –
You guessed – from the way the sentence toiled –
You could hear the Bodice tug, behind you –
As if it held but the might of a child –
You almost pitied it – you – it worked so –
Tell Him – no – you may quibble there –
For it would split His Heart, to know it –
And then you and I, were silenter.

Tell Him – Night finished – before we finished –
And the Old Clock kept neighing "Day"!
And you – got sleepy – and begged to be ended –
What could it hinder so – to say?
Tell Him – just how she sealed you – Cautious!
But – if He ask where you are hid
Until tomorrow – Happy letter!
Gesture Coquette – and shake your Head!

c. 1862   *1891*

I envy Seas, whereon He rides –
I envy Spokes of Wheels

Of Chariots, that Him convey –
I envy Crooked Hills

That gaze upon His journey –
How easy All can see
What is forbidden utterly
As Heaven – unto me!

I envy Nests of Sparrows –
That dot His distant Eaves –
The wealthy Fly, upon His Pane –
The happy – happy Leaves –

That just abroad His Window
Have Summer's leave to play –
The Ear Rings of Pizarro
Could not obtain for me –

I envy Light – that wakes Him –
And Bells – that boldly ring
To tell Him it is Noon, abroad –
Myself – be Noon to Him –

Yet interdict – my Blossom –
And abrogate – my Bee –
Lest Noon in Everlasting Night –
Drop Gabriel – and Me –

c. 1862   1896

201
(500)
Within my Garden, rides a Bird
Upon a single Wheel –
Whose spokes a dizzy Music make
As 'twere a travelling Mill –

He never stops, but slackens
Above the Ripest Rose –
Partakes without alighting
And praises as he goes,

Till every spice is tasted –
And then his Fairy Gig
Reels in remoter atmospheres –
And I rejoin my Dog,

And He and I, perplex us
If positive, 'twere we –
Or bore the Garden in the Brain
This Curiosity –

But He, the best Logician,
Refers my clumsy eye –
To just vibrating Blossoms!
An Exquisite Reply!

c. 1862   *1929*

202
(501)
This World is not Conclusion.
A Species stands beyond –
Invisible, as Music –
But positive, as Sound –
It beckons, and it baffles –
Philosophy – don't know –
And through a Riddle, at the last –
Sagacity, must go –
To guess it, puzzles scholars –
To gain it, Men have borne
Contempt of Generations
And Crucifixion, shown –

[123]

Faith slips – and laughs, and rallies –
Blushes, if any see –
Plucks at a twig of Evidence –
And asks a Vane, the way –
Much Gesture, from the Pulpit –
Strong Hallelujahs roll –
Narcotics cannot still the Tooth
That nibbles at the soul –

c. 1862   *1896*

203
(508)

I'm ceded – I've stopped being Theirs –
The name They dropped upon my face
With water, in the country church
Is finished using, now,
And They can put it with my Dolls,
My childhood, and the string of spools,
I've finished threading – too –

Baptized, before, without the choice,
But this time, consciously, of Grace –
Unto supremest name –
Called to my Full – The Crescent dropped –
Existence's whole Arc, filled up,
With one small Diadem.

My second Rank – too small the first –
Crowned – Crowing – on my Father's breast –
A half unconscious Queen –
But this time – Adequate – Erect,
With Will to choose, or to reject,
And I choose, just a Crown –

c. 1862   *1890*

It was not Death, for I stood up,
And all the Dead, lie down –
It was not Night, for all the Bells
Put out their Tongues, for Noon.

It was not Frost, for on my Flesh
I felt Siroccos – crawl –
Nor Fire – for just my Marble feet
Could keep a Chancel, cool –

And yet, it tasted, like them all,
The Figures I have seen
Set orderly, for Burial,
Reminded me, of mine –

As if my life were shaven,
And fitted to a frame,
And could not breathe without a key,
And 'twas like Midnight, some –

When everything that ticked – has stopped –
And Space stares all around –
Or Grisly frosts – first Autumn morns,
Repeal the Beating Ground –

But, most, like Chaos – Stopless – cool –
Without a Chance, or Spar –
Or even a Report of Land –
To justify – Despair.

c. *1862*   *1891*

If you were coming in the Fall,
I'd brush the Summer by

[125]

With half a smile, and half a spurn,
As Housewives do, a Fly.

If I could see you in a year,
I'd wind the months in balls –
And put them each in separate Drawers,
For fear the numbers fuse –

If only Centuries, delayed,
I'd count them on my Hand,
Subtracting, till my fingers dropped
Into Van Dieman's Land.

If certain, when this life was out –
That yours and mine, should be
I'd toss it yonder, like a Rind,
And take Eternity –

But, now, uncertain of the length
Of this, that is between,
It goads me, like the Goblin Bee –
That will not state – its sting.

c. 1862   *1890*

206
(512)

The Soul has Bandaged moments –
When too appalled to stir –
She feels some ghastly Fright come up
And stop to look at her –

Salute her – with long fingers –
Caress her freezing hair –
Sip, Goblin, from the very lips
The Lover – hovered – o'er –

[126]

Unworthy, that a thought so mean
Accost a Theme – so – fair –

The soul has moments of Escape –
When bursting all the doors –
She dances like a Bomb, abroad,
And swings upon the Hours,

As do the Bee – delirious borne –
Long Dungeoned from his Rose –
Touch Liberty – then know no more,
But Noon, and Paradise –

The Soul's retaken moments –
When, Felon led along,
With shackles on the plumed feet,
And staples, in the Song,

The Horror welcomes her, again,
These, are not brayed of Tongue –

c. 1862   *1945*

207
(515)
No Crowd that has occurred
Exhibit – I suppose
That General Attendance
That Resurrection – does –

Circumference be full –
The long restricted Grave
Assert her Vital Privilege –
The Dust – connect – and live –

On Atoms – features place –
All Multitudes that were

[127]

Efface in the Comparison –
As Suns – dissolve a star –

Solemnity – prevail –
Its Individual Doom
Possess each separate Consciousness –
August – Absorbed – Numb –

What Duplicate – exist –
What Parallel can be –
Of the Significance of This –
To Universe – and Me?

c. 1862   *1929*

208
(516)
Beauty – be not caused – It Is –
Chase it, and it ceases –
Chase it not, and it abides –

Overtake the Creases

In the Meadow – when the Wind
Runs his fingers thro' it –
Deity will see to it
That You never do it –

c. 1862   *1929*

209
(520)
I started Early – Took my Dog –
And visited the Sea –

The Mermaids in the Basement
Came out to look at me –

And Frigates – in the Upper Floor
Extended Hempen Hands –
Presuming Me to be a Mouse –
Aground – upon the Sands –

But no Man moved Me – till the Tide
Went past my simple Shoe –
And past my Apron – and my Belt
And past my Bodice – too –

And made as He would eat me up ·-
As wholly as a Dew
Upon a Dandelion's Sleeve –
And then – I started – too –

And He – He followed – close behind –
I felt His Silver Heel
Upon my Ankle – Then my Shoes
Would overflow with Pearl –

Until We met the Solid Town –
No One He seemed to know –
And bowing – with a Mighty look –
At me – The Sea withdrew –

c. 1862   1891

210
(523)

Sweet – You forgot – but I remembered
Every time   for Two –
So that the Sum be never hindered
Through Decay of You –

Say if I erred? Accuse my Farthings –
Blame the little Hand
Happy it be for You – a Beggar's –
Seeking More – to spend –

Just to be Rich – to waste my Guineas
On so Best a Heart –
Just to be Poor – for Barefoot Vision
You – Sweet – Shut me out –

c. 1862   *1945*

211
(526)

To hear an Oriole sing
May be a common thing –
Or only a divine.

It is not of the Bird
Who sings the same, unheard,
As unto Crowd –

The Fashion of the Ear
Attireth that it hear
In Dun, or fair –

So whether it be Rune,
Or whether it be none
Is of within.

The "Tune is in the Tree –"
The Skeptic – showeth me –
"No Sir! In Thee!"

c. 1862   *1891*

212
(528)

Mine – by the Right of the White Election!
Mine – by the Royal Seal!
Mine – by the Sign in the Scarlet prison –
Bars – cannot conceal!

Mine – here – in Vision – and in Veto!
Mine – by the Grave's Repeal –
Titled – Confirmed –
Delirious Charter!
Mine – long as Ages steal!

c. 1862   *1890*

213
(529)

I'm sorry for the Dead – Today –
It's such congenial times
Old Neighbors have at fences –
It's time o' year for Hay.

And Broad – Sunburned Acquaintance
Discourse between the Toil –
And laugh, a homely species
That makes the Fences smile –

It seems so straight to lie away
From all the noise of Fields –
The Busy Carts – the fragrant Cocks –
The Mower's Metre – Steals

A Trouble lest they're homesick –
Those Farmers – and their Wives –
Set separate from the Farming –
And all the Neighbors' lives –

[131]

A Wonder if the Sepulchre
Don't feel a lonesome way --
When Men – and Boys – and Carts – and June,
Go down the Fields to "Hay" –

1929

214
(530)

You cannot put a Fire out –
A Thing that can ignite
Can go, itself, without a Fan –
Upon the slowest Night –

You cannot fold a Flood –
And put it in a Drawer –
Because the Winds would find it out –
And tell your Cedar Floor –

c. 1862   *1896*

215
(531)

We dream – it is good we are dreaming –
It would hurt us – were we awake –
But since it is playing – kill us,
And we are playing – shriek –

What harm? Men die – externally –
It is a truth – of Blood –
But we – are dying in Drama –
And Drama – is never dead –

[132]

Cautious – We jar each other –
And either – open the eyes –
Lest the Phantasm – prove the Mistake –
And the livid Surprise

Cool us to Shafts of Granite –
With just an Age – and Name –
And perhaps a phrase in Egyptian –
It's prudenter – to dream –

c. 1862   *1935*

216
(533)

Two Butterflies went out at Noon –
And waltzed upon a Farm –
Then stepped straight through the Firmament
And rested, on a Beam –

And then – together bore away
Upon a shining Sea –
Though never yet, in any Port –
Their coming, mentioned – be –

If spoken by the distant Bird –
If met in Ether Sea
By Frigate, or by Merchantman –
No notice – was – to me –

c. 1862   *1891*

217
(536)
The Heart asks Pleasure – first –
And then – Excuse from Pain –

[133]

And then – those little Anodynes
That deaden suffering –

And then – to go to sleep –
And then – if it should be
The will of its Inquisitor
The privilege to die –

c. 1862   1890

218
(537)

Me prove it now – Whoever doubt
Me stop to prove it – now –
Make haste – the Scruple! Death be scant
For Opportunity –

The River reaches to my feet –
As yet – My Heart be dry –
Oh Lover – Life could not convince –
Might Death – enable Thee –

The River reaches to My Breast –
Still – still – My Hands above
Proclaim with their remaining Might –
Dost recognize the Love?

The River reaches to my Mouth –
Remember – when the Sea
Swept by my searching eyes – the last –
Themselves were quick – with Thee!

c. 1862   1935

219
(539)

The Province of the Saved
Should be the Art – To save –
Through Skill obtained in Themselves –
The Science of the Grave

No Man can understand
But He that hath endured
The Dissolution – in Himself –
That Man – be qualified

To qualify Despair
To Those who failing new –
Mistake Defeat for Death – Each time –
Till acclimated – to –

c. 1862   *1935*

220
(540)

I took my Power in my Hand –
And went against the World –
'Twas not so much as David – had –
But I – was twice as bold –

I aimed my Pebble – but Myself
Was all the one that fell –
Was it Goliah – was too large –
Or was myself – too small?

c 1862   *1891*

221
(543)
I fear a Man of frugal Speech –
I fear a Silent Man –
Haranguer – I can overtake –
Or Babbler – entertain –

But He who weigheth – While the Rest –
Expend their furthest pound –
Of this Man – I am wary –
I fear that He is Grand –

ᴄ. *1862*   1929

222
(544)
The Martyr Poets – did not tell –
But wrought their Pang in syllable –
That when their mortal name be numb –
Their mortal fate – encourage Some –

The Martyr Painters – never spoke –
Bequeathing – rather – to their Work –
That when their conscious fingers cease –
Some seek in Art – the Art of Peace –

c. *1862*   *1935*

223
(546)
To fill a Gap
Insert the Thing that caused it –

Block it up
With Other – and 'twill yawn the more –
You cannot solder an Abyss
With Air.

c. 1862   1929

224
(547)

I've seen a Dying Eye
Run round and round a Room –
In search of Something – as it seemed –
Then Cloudier become –
And then – obscure with Fog –
And then – be soldered down
Without disclosing what it be
'Twere blessed to have seen –

c. 1862   1890

225
(548)

Death is potential to that Man
Who dies – and to his friend –
Beyond that – unconspicuous
To Anyone but God –

Of these Two – God remembers
The longest – for the friend –
Is integral – and therefore
Itself dissolved – of God –

c. 1862   1945

226
(549)

That I did always love
I bring thee Proof
That till I loved
I never lived – Enough –

That I shall love alway –
I argue thee
That love is life –
And life hath Immortality –

This – dost thou doubt – Sweet –
Then have I
Nothing to show
But Calvary –

c. 1862   *189c*

227
(552)

An ignorance a Sunset
Confer upon the Eye –
Of Territory – Color –
Circumference – Decay –

Its Amber Revelation
Exhilarate – Debase –
Omnipotence' inspection
Of Our inferior face –

And when the solemn features
Confirm – in Victory –
We start – as if detected
In Immortality –

c. 1862   *1935*

228
(553)

One Crucifixion is recorded – only --
How many be
Is not affirmed of Mathematics –
Or History –

One Calvary – exhibited to Stranger –
As many be
As persons – or Peninsulas –
Gethsemane –

Is but a Province – in the Being's Centre –
Judea –
For Journey – or Crusade's Achieving –
Too near –

Our Lord – indeed – made Compound Witness –
And yet –
There's newer – nearer Crucifixion
Than That –

c. 1862   1945

229
(560)

It knew no lapse, nor Diminution –
But large – serene –
Burned on – until through Dissolution –
It failed from Men –

I could not deem these Planetary forces
Annulled –
But suffered an Exchange of Territory –
Or World –

c. 1862   1945

I measure every Grief I meet
With narrow, probing, Eyes –
I wonder if It weighs like Mine –
Or has an Easier size.

I wonder if They bore it long –
Or did it just begin –
I could not tell the Date of Mine –
It feels so old a pain –

I wonder if it hurts to live –
And if They have to try –
And whether – could They choose between –
It would not be – to die –

I note that Some – gone patient long –
At length, renew their smile –
An imitation of a Light
That has so little Oil –

I wonder if when Years have piled –
Some Thousands – on the Harm –
That hurt them early – such a lapse
Could give them any Balm –

Or would they go on aching still
Through Centuries of Nerve –
Enlightened to a larger Pain –
In Contrast with the Love –

The Grieved – are many – I am told –
There is the various Cause –
Death – is but one – and comes but once –
And only nails the eyes –

There's Grief of Want – and Grief of Cold –
A sort they call "Despair" –

There's Banishment from native Eyes —
In sight of Native Air —

And though I may not guess the kind —
Correctly — yet to me
A piercing Comfort it affords
In passing Calvary —

To note the fashions — of the Cross —
And how they're mostly worn —
Still fascinated to presume
That Some — are like My Own —

c. 1862   1896

231
(564)

My period had come for Prayer —
No other Art — would do —
My Tactics missed a rudiment —
Creator — Was it you?

God grows above — so those who pray
Horizons — must ascend —
And so I stepped upon the North
To see this Curious Friend —

His House was not — no sign had He —
By Chimney — nor by Door
Could I infer his Residence —
Vast Prairies of Air

Unbroken by a Settler —
Were all that I could see —
Infinitude — Had'st Thou no Face
That I might look on Thee?

[141]

The Silence condescended –
Creation stopped – for Me –
But awed beyond my errand –
I worshipped – did not "pray" –

c. 1862   *1929*

232
(565)

One Anguish – in a Crowd –
A Minor thing – it sounds –
And yet, unto the single Doe
Attempted of the Hounds

'Tis Terror as consummate
As Legions of Alarm
Did leap, full flanked, upon the Host –
'Tis Units – make the Swarm –

A Small Leech – on the Vitals –
The sliver, in the Lung –
The Bung out – of an Artery –
Are scarce accounted – Harms –

Yet mighty – by relation
To that Repealless thing –
A Being – impotent to end –
When once it has begun –

c. 1862   *1945*

233
(566)

A Dying Tiger – moaned for Drink –
I hunted all the Sand –

I caught the Dripping of a Rock
And bore it in my Hand –

His Mighty Balls – in death were thick –
But searching – I could see
A Vision on the Retina
Of Water – and of me –

'Twas not my blame – who sped too slow –
'Twas not his blame – who died
While I was reaching him –
But 'twas – the fact that He was dead –

c. *1862*   *1945*

234
(567)

He gave away his Life –
To Us – Gigantic Sum –
A trifle – in his own esteem –
But magnified – by Fame –

Until it burst the Hearts
That fancied they could hold –
When swift it slipped its limit –
And on the Heavens – unrolled –

'Tis Ours – to wince – and weep –
And wonder – and decay
By Blossoms gradual process –
He chose – Maturity –

And quickening – as we sowed –
Just obviated Bud –
And when We turned to note the Growth –
Broke – perfect – from the Pod –

c. *1862*   *1935*

We learned the Whole of Love –
The Alphabet – the Words –
A Chapter – then the mighty Book –
Then – Revelation closed –

But in Each Other's eyes
An Ignorance beheld –
Diviner than the Childhood's –
And each to each, a Child –

Attempted to expound
What Neither – understood –
Alas, that Wisdom is so large –
And Truth – so manifold!

≈. 1862

1945

I reckon – when I count at all –
First – Poets – Then the Sun –
Then Summer – Then the Heaven of God –
And then – the List is done –

But, looking back – the First so seems
To Comprehend the Whole –
The Others look a needless Show –
So I write – Poets – All –

Their Summer – lasts a Solid Year –
They can afford a Sun
The East – would deem extravagant –
And if the Further Heaven –

Be Beautiful as they prepare
For Those who worship Them –
It is too difficult a Grace –
To justify the Dream –

c. 1862   1929

237
(571)

Must be a Woe –
A loss or so –
To bend the eye
Best Beauty's way –

But – once aslant
It notes Delight
As difficult
As Stalactite

A Common Bliss
Were had for less –
The price – is
Even as the Grace –

Our lord – thought no
Extravagance
To pay – a Cross –

c. 1862   1935

238
(575)

"Heaven" has different Signs – to me –
Sometimes, I think that Noon

Is but a symbol of the Place –
And when again, at Dawn,

A mighty look runs round the World
And settles in the Hills –
An Awe if it should be like that
Upon the Ignorance steals –

The Orchard, when the Sun is on –
The Triumph of the Birds
When they together Victory make –
Some Carnivals of Clouds –

The Rapture of a finished Day –
Returning to the West –
All these – remind us of the place
That Men call "Paradise" –

Itself be fairer – we suppose –
But how Ourself, shall be
Adorned, for a Superior Grace –
Not yet, our eyes can see –

c. 1862   *1929*

239
(578)

The Body grows without –
The more convenient way –
That if the Spirit – like to hide
Its Temple stands, alway,

Ajar – secure – inviting –
It never did betray
The Soul that asked its shelter
In solemn honesty

c. 1862   *1891*

240
(579)

I had been hungry, all the Years –
My Noon had Come – to dine –
I trembling drew the Table near –
And touched the Curious Wine –

'Twas this on Tables I had seen –
When turning, hungry, Home
I looked in Windows, for the Wealth
I could not hope – for Mine –

I did not know the ample Bread –
'Twas so unlike the Crumb
The Birds and I, had often shared
In Nature's – Dining Room –

The Plenty hurt me – 'twas so new –
Myself felt ill – and odd –
As Berry – of a Mountain Bush –
Transplanted – to the Road –

Nor was I hungry – so I found
That Hunger – was a way
Of Persons outside Windows –
The Entering – takes away –

c. 1862   1891

241
(582)

Inconceivably solemn!
Things so gay
Pierce – by the very Press
Of Imagery –

[147]

Their far Parades – order on the eye
With a mute Pomp –
A pleading Pageantry –

Flags, are a brave sight –
But no true Eye
Ever went by One –
Steadily –

Music's triumphant –
But the fine Ear
Winces with delight
Are Drums too near –

c. 1862

1929

242
(583)

A Toad, can die of Light –
Death is the Common Right
Of Toads and Men –
Of Earl and Midge
The privilege –
Why swagger, then?
The Gnat's supremacy is large as Thine –

Life – is a different Thing –
So measure Wine –
Naked of Flask – Naked of Cask –
Bare Rhine –
Which Ruby's mine?

1862

1896

I like to see it lap the Miles –
And lick the Valleys up –
And stop to feed itself at Tanks –
And then – prodigious step

Around a Pile of Mountains –
And supercilious peer
In Shanties – by the sides of Roads –
And then a Quarry pare

To fit its Ribs
And crawl between
Complaining all the while
In horrid – hooting stanza –
Then chase itself down Hill –

And neigh like Boanerges –
Then – punctual as a Star
Stop – docile and omnipotent
At its own stable door –

c. 1862   *1891*

244
(591)

To interrupt His Yellow Plan
The Sun does not allow
Caprices of the Atmosphere –
And even when the Snow

Heaves Balls of Specks, like Vicious Boy
Directly in His Eye –
Does not so much as turn His Head
Busy with Majesty –

'Tis His to stimulate the Earth –
And magnetize the Sea –
And bind Astronomy, in place,
Yet Any passing by

Would deem Ourselves – the busier
As the Minutest Bee
That rides – emits a Thunder –
A Bomb – to justify –

c. 1862   *1929*

245
(592)

What care the Dead, for Chanticleer –
What care the Dead for Day?
'Tis late your Sunrise vex their face –
And Purple Ribaldry – of Morning

Pour as blank on them
As on the Tier of Wall
The Mason builded, yesterday,
And equally as cool –

What care the Dead for Summer?
The Solstice had no Sun
Could waste the Snow before their Gate –
And knew One Bird a Tune –

Could thrill their Mortised Ear
Of all the Birds that be –
This One – beloved of Mankind
Henceforward cherished be –

What care the Dead for Winter?
Themselves as easy freeze --

June Noon – as January Night –
As soon the South – her Breeze

Of Sycamore – or Cinnamon –
Deposit in a Stone
And put a Stone to keep it Warm –
Give Spices – unto Men –

c. 1862   1932

246
(594)
The Battle fought between the Soul
And No Man – is the One
Of all the Battles prevalent –
By far the Greater One –

No News of it is had abroad –
Its Bodiless Campaign
Establishes, and terminates –
Invisible – Unknown –

Nor History – record it –
As Legions of a Night
The Sunrise scatters – These endure –
Enact – and terminate –

c. 1862   1929

247
(J90)
Three times – we parted – Breath – and I –
Three times – He would not go –

But strove to stir the lifeless Fan
The Waters – strove to stay.

Three Times – the Billows tossed me up –
Then caught me – like a Ball –
Then made Blue faces in my face –
And pushed away a sail

That crawled Leagues off – I liked to see –
For thinking – while I die –
How pleasant to behold a Thing
Where Human faces – be –

The Waves grew sleepy – Breath – did not –
The Winds – like Children – lulled –
Then Sunrise kissed my Chrysalis –
And I stood up – and lived –

c. 1862   1929

248
(599)
There is a pain – so utter –
It swallows substance up –
Then covers the Abyss with Trance –
So Memory can step
Around – across – upon it –
As one within a Swoon –
Goes safely – where an open eye –
Would drop Him – Bone by Bone.

c. 1862   1929

[152]

Unto my Books – so good to turn –
Far ends of tired Days –
It half endears the Abstinence –
And Pain – is missed – in Praise –

As Flavors – cheer Retarded Guests
With Banquettings to be –
So Spices – stimulate the time
Till my small Library –

It may be Wilderness – without –
Far feet of failing Men –
But Holiday – excludes the night –
And it is Bells – within –

I thank these Kinsmen of the Shelf –
Their Countenances Kid
Enamor – in Prospective –
And satisfy – obtained –

c. 1862   *1891*

Of nearness to her sundered Things
The Soul has special times –
When Dimness – looks the Oddity –
Distinctness – easy – seems –

The Shapes we buried, dwell about,
Familiar, in the Rooms –
Untarnished by the Sepulchre,
The Mouldering Playmate comes –

In just the Jacket that he wore –
Long buttoned in the Mold
Since we – old mornings, Children – played –
Divided – by a world –

The Grave yields back her Robberies –
The Years, our pilfered Things –
Bright Knots of Apparitions
Salute us, with their wings –

As we – it were – that perished –
Themself – had just remained till we rejoin them –
And 'twas they, and not ourself
That mourned.

c. 1862   *1929*

251
(608)

Afraid! Of whom am I afraid?
Not Death – for who is He?
The Porter of my Father's Lodge
As much abasheth me!

Of Life? 'Twere odd I fear [a] thing
That comprehendeth me
In one or two existences –
As Deity decree –

Of Resurrection? Is the East
Afraid to trust the Morn
With her fastidious forehead?
As soon impeach my Crown!

c. 1862   *1890*

1 Years had been from Home
And now before the Door
I dared not enter, lest a Face
I never saw before

Stare stolid into mine
And ask my Business there –
"My Business but a Life I left
Was such remaining there?"

I leaned upon the Awe –
I lingered with Before –
The Second like an Ocean rolled
And broke against my ear –

I laughed a crumbling Laugh
That I could fear a Door
Who Consternation compassed
And never winced before.

I fitted to the Latch
My Hand, with trembling care
Lest back the awful Door should spring
And leave me in the Floor –

Then moved my Fingers off
As cautiously as Glass
And held my ears, and like a Thief
Fled gasping from the House –

c. 1872   *1891*

I see thee better – in the Dark –
I do not need a Light –

The Love of Thee – a Prism be –
Excelling Violet –

I see thee better for the Years
That hunch themselves between –
The Miner's Lamp – sufficient be –
To nullify the Mine –

And in the Grave – I see Thee best –
Its little Panels be
Aglow – All ruddy – with the Light
I held so high, for Thee –

What need of Day –
To Those whose Dark – hath so – surpassing Sun –
It deem it be – Continually –
At the Meridian?

c. *1862*   *1914*

254
(612)

It would have starved a Gnat –
To live so small as I –
And yet I was a living Child –
With Food's necessity

Upon me – like a Claw –
I could no more remove
Than I could coax a Leech away –
Or make a Dragon – move –

Nor like the Gnat – had I –
The privilege to fly
And seek a Dinner for myself –
How mightier He – than I –

Nor like Himself – the Art
Upon the Window Pane
To gad my little Being out –
And not begin – again –

c. 1862   1945

255
(615)

Our journey had advanced –
Our feet were almost come
To that odd Fork in Being's Road –
Eternity – by Term –

Our pace took sudden awe –
Our feet – reluctant – led –
Before – were Cities – but Between –
The Forest of the Dead –

Retreat – was out of Hope –
Behind – a Sealed Route –
Eternity's White Flag – Before –
And God – at every Gate –

c. 1862   1891

256
(618)

At leisure is the Soul
That gets a Staggering Blow –
The Width of Life – before it spreads
Without a thing to do –

[157]

It begs you give it Work –
But just the placing Pins –
Or humblest Patchwork – Children do –
To Help its Vacant Hands –

c. 1862   *1929*

257
(621)

I asked no other thing –
No other – was denied –
I offered Being – for it –
The Mighty Merchant sneered –

Brazil? He twirled a Button –
Without a glance my way –
"But – Madam – is there nothing else –
That We can show – Today?"

c. 1862   *1890*

258
(624)

Forever – is composed of Nows –
'Tis not a different time –
Except for Infiniteness –
And Latitude of Home –

From this – experienced Here –
Remove the Dates – to These –
Let Months dissolve in further Months –
And Years – exhale in Years –

[158]

Without Debate – or Pause –
Or Celebrated Days –
No different Our Years would be
From Anno Domini's –

c. 1862   1929

259
(625)

'Twas a long Parting – but the time
For Interview – had Come –
Before the Judgment Seat of God –
The last – and second time

These Fleshless Lovers met –
A Heaven in a Gaze –
A Heaven of Heavens – the Privilege
Of one another's Eyes –

No Lifetime – on Them –
Appareled as the new
Unborn – except They had beheld –
Born infiniter – now –

Was Bridal – e'er like This?
A Paradise – the Host –
And Cherubim – and Seraphim –
The unobtrusive Guest –

c. 1862   1890

260
(627)

The Tint I cannot take – is best
The Color too remote

That I could show it in Bazaar –
A Guinea at a sight –

The fine – impalpable Array –
That swaggers on the eye
Like Cleopatra's Company –
Repeated – in the sky –

The Moments of Dominion
That happen on the Soul
And leave it with a Discontent
Too exquisite – to tell –

The eager look – on Landscapes –
As if they just repressed
Some Secret – that was pushing
Like Chariots – in the Vest –

The Pleading of the Summer –
That other Prank – of Snow –
That Cushions Mystery with Tulle,
For fear the Squirrels – know.

Their Graspless manners – mock us –
Until the Cheated Eye
Shuts arrogantly – in the Grave –
Another way – to see –

c. 1862   *1929*

261
(630)
The Lightning playeth – all the while –
But when He singeth – then –
Ourselves are conscious He exist –
And we approach Him – stern –

[160]

With Insulators – and a Glove –
Whose short – sepulchral Bass
Alarms us – tho' His Yellow feet
May pass – and counterpass –

Upon the Ropes – above our Head –
Continual – with the News –
Nor We so much as check our speech –
Nor stop to cross Ourselves –

c. 1862   1945

262
(632)

The Brain – is wider than the Sky –
For – put them side by side –
The one the other will contain
With ease – and You – beside –

The Brain is deeper than the sea –
For – hold them – Blue to Blue –
The one the other will absorb –
As Sponges – Buckets – do –

The Brain is just the weight of God –
For – Heft them – Pound for Pound –
And they will differ – if they do –
As Syllable from Sound –

c. 1862   1896

263
(633)

When Bells stop ringing – Church – begins –
The Positive – of Bells –

[161]

When Cogs – stop – that's Circumference –
The Ultimate – of Wheels.

c. 1862   1945

264
(636)

The Way I read a Letter's – this –
'Tis first – I lock the Door –
And push it with my fingers – next –
For transport it be sure –

And then I go the furthest off
To counteract a knock –
Then draw my little Letter forth
And slowly pick the lock –

Then – glancing narrow, at the Wall –
And narrow at the floor
For firm Conviction of a Mouse
Not exorcised before –

Peruse how infinite I am
To no one that You – know –
And sigh for lack of Heaven – but not
The Heaven God bestow –

c. 1862   1891

265
(640)

I cannot live with You –
It would be Life –

And Life is over there –
Behind the Shelf

The Sexton keeps the Key to –
Putting up
Our Life – His Porcelain –
Like a Cup –

Discarded of the Housewife –
Quaint – or Broke –
A newer Sevres pleases –
Old Ones crack –

I could not die – with You –
For One must wait
To shut the Other's Gaze down –
You – could not –

And I – Could I stand by
And see You – freeze –
Without my Right of Frost –
Death's privilege?

Nor could I rise – with You –
Because Your Face
Would put out Jesus' –
That New Grace

Glow plain – and foreign
On my homesick Eye –
Except that You than He
Shone closer by –

They'd judge Us – How –
For You served Heaven – You know,
Or sought to –
I could not –

Because You saturated Sight –
And I had no more Eyes
For sordid excellence
As Paradise

And were You lost, I would be –
Though My Name
Rang loudest
On the Heavenly fame –

And were You – saved –
And I – condemned to be
Where You were not –
That self – were Hell to Me –

So We must meet apart –
You there – I – here –
With just the Door ajar
That Oceans are – and Prayer –
And that White Sustenance –
Despair –

c. *1862*   *1890*

266
(641)

Size circumscribes – it has no room
For petty furniture –
The Giant tolerates no Gnat
For Ease of Gianture –

Repudiates it, all the more –
Because intrinsic size
Ignores the possibility
Of Calumnies – or Flies.

c. *1862*   *1935*

[164]

267
(642)

Me from Myself – to banish –
Had I Art –
Impregnable my Fortress
Unto All Heart –

But since Myself – assault Me –
How have I peace
Except by subjugating
Consciousness?

And since We're mutual Monarch
How this be
Except by Abdication –
Me – of Me?

c. 1862

1929

268
(645)

Bereavement in their death to feel
Whom We have never seen –
A Vital Kinsmanship import
Our Soul and theirs – between –

For Stranger – Strangers do not mourn –
There be Immortal friends
Whom Death see first – 'tis news of this
That paralyze Ourselves –

Who, vital only to Our Thought –
Such Presence bear away
In dying   'tis as if Our Souls
Absconded – suddenly –

c. 1862

1935

269
(650)

Pain – has an Element of Blank –
It cannot recollect
When it begun – or if there were
A time when it was not –

It has no Future – but itself –
Its Infinite contain
Its Past – enlightened to perceive
New Periods – of Pain.

c. 1862   1890

270
(657)

I dwell in Possibility –
A fairer House than Prose –
More numerous of Windows –
Superior – for Doors –

Of Chambers as the Cedars –
Impregnable of Eye –
And for an Everlasting Roof
The Gambrels of the Sky –

Of Visitors – the fairest –
For Occupation – This –
The spreading wide my narrow Hands
To gather Paradise –

c. 1862   1929

Of all the Souls that stand create –
I have elected – One –
When Sense from Spirit – files away –
And Subterfuge – is done –
When that which is – and that which was –
Apart – intrinsic – stand –
And this brief Drama in the flesh –
Is shifted – like a Sand –
When Figures show their royal Front –
And Mists – are carved away,
Behold the Atom – I preferred –
To all the lists of Clay!

c. 1862   *1891*

Bloom upon the Mountain – stated –
Blameless of a Name –
Efflorescence of a Sunset –
Reproduced – the same –

Seed, had I, my Purple Sowing
Should endow the Day –
Not a Tropic of a Twilight –
Show itself away –

Who for tilling – to the Mountain
Come, and disappear –
Whose be Her Renown, or fading,
Witness, is not here –

[167]

While I state – the Solemn Petals,
Far as North – and East,
Far as South and West – expanding –
Culminate – in Rest –

And the Mountain to the Evening
Fit His Countenance –
Indicating, by no Muscle –
The Experience –

c. 1863   *1914*

273
(668)

"Nature" is what we see –
The Hill – the Afternoon –
Squirrel – Eclipse – the Bumble bee –
Nay – Nature is Heaven –
Nature is what we hear –
The Bobolink – the Sea –
Thunder – the Cricket –
Nay – Nature is Harmony –
Nature is what we know –
Yet have no art to say –
So impotent Our Wisdom is
To her Simplicity.

c. 1863   *1914*

274
(670)

One need not be a Chamber – to be Haunted –
One need not be a House –

[168]

The Brain has Corridors – surpassing
Material Place –

Far safer, of a Midnight Meeting
External Ghost
Than its interior Confronting –
That Cooler Host.

Far safer, through an Abbey gallop,
The Stones a'chase –
Than Unarmed, one's a'self encounter –
In lonesome Place –

Ourself behind ourself, concealed –
Should startle most –
Assassin hid in our Apartment
Be Horror's least.

The Body – borrows a Revolver –
He bolts the Door –
O'erlooking a superior spectre –
Or More –

c. 1863   *1891*

275
(672)

The Future – never spoke –
Nor will He – like the Dumb –
Reveal by sign – a syllable
Of His Profound To Come –

But when the News be ripe –
Presents it – in the Act –
Forestalling Preparation –
Escape – or Substitute –

[169]

Indifferent to Him –
The Dower – as the Doom –
His Office – but to execute
Fate's – Telegram – to Him –

c. 1863

1914

276
(673)
The Love a Life can show Below
Is but a filament, I know,
Of that diviner thing
That faints upon the face of Noon –
And smites the Tinder in the Sun –
And hinders Gabriel's Wing –

'Tis this – in Music – hints and sways –
And far abroad on Summer days –
Distils uncertain pain –
'Tis this enamors in the East –
And tints the Transit in the West
With harrowing Iodine –

'Tis this – invites – appalls – endows –
Flits – glimmers – proves – dissolves –
Returns – suggests – convicts – enchants –
Then – flings in Paradise –

c. 1863

1929

277
(674)
The Soul that hath a Guest
Doth seldom go abroad –

Diviner Crowd at Home –
Obliterate the need –

And Courtesy forbid
A Host's departure when
Upon Himself be visiting
The Emperor of Men –

c. *1863*   *1914*

278
(675)
Essential Oils – are wrung –
The Attar from the Rose
Be not expressed by Suns – alone –
It is the gift of Screws –

The General Rose – decay –
But this – in Lady's Drawer
Make Summer – When the Lady lie
In Ceaseless Rosemary –

c. *1863*   *1891*

279
(679)
Conscious am I in my Chamber,
Of a 'shapeless friend –
He doth not attest by Posture –
Nor Confirm – by Word –

Neither Place – need I present Him –
Fitter Courtesy

[171]

Hospitable intuition
Of His Company –

Presence – is His furthest license –
Neither He to Me
Nor Myself to Him – by Accent –
Forfeit Probity –

Weariness of Him, were quainter
Than Monotony
Knew a Particle – of Space's
Vast Society –

Neither if He visit Other –
Do He dwell – or Nay – know I –
But Instinct esteem Him
Immortality –

c. 1863   *1929*

280
(680)

Each Life Converges to some Centre –
Expressed – or still –
Exists in every Human Nature
A Goal –

Embodied scarcely to itself – it may be –
Too fair
For Credibility's presumption
To mar –

Adored with caution – as a Brittle Heaven –
To reach
Were hopeless, as the Rainbow's Raiment
To touch –

[172]

Yet persevered toward – surer – for the Distance –
How high –
Unto the Saints' slow diligence –
The Sky –

Ungained – it may be – by a Life's low Venture –
But then –
Eternity enable the endeavoring
Again.

c. 1863   1891

281
(682)

'Twould ease – a Butterfly –
Elate – a Bee –
Thou'rt neither –
Neither – thy capacity –

But, Blossom, were I,
I would rather be
Thy moment
Than a Bee's Eternity –

Content of fading
Is enough for me –
Fade I unto Divinity –

And Dying – Lifetime –
Ample as the Eye –
Her least attention raise on me –

c. 1863   1945

282
(683)

The Soul unto itself
Is an imperial friend –
Or the most agonizing Spy –
An Enemy – could send –

Secure against its own –
No treason it can fear –
Itself – its Sovereign – of itself
The Soul should stand in Awe –

c. 1862   *1891*

283
(686)

They say that "Time assuages" –
Time never did assuage –
An actual suffering strengthens
As Sinews do, with age –

Time is a Test of Trouble –
But not a Remedy –
If such it prove, it prove too
There was no Malady –

c. 1863   *1896*

284
(695)

As if the Sea should part
And show a further Sea –

[174]

And that – a further – and the Three
But a presumption be –

Of Periods of Seas –
Unvisited of Shores –
Themselves the Verge of Seas to be –
Eternity – is Those –

c. *1863*   *1929*

285
(701)

A Thought went up my mind today –
That I have had before –
But did not finish – some way back –
I could not fix the Year –

Nor where it went – nor why it came
The second time to me –
Nor definitely, what it was –
Have I the Art to say –

But somewhere – in my Soul – I know –
I've met the Thing before –
It just reminded me – 'twas all –
And came my way no more –

c. *1863*   *1891*

286
(703)

Out of sight? What of that?
See the Bird – reach it!

Curve by Curve – Sweep by Sweep –
Round the Steep Air –
Danger! What is that to Her?
Better 'tis to fail – there –
Than debate – here –

Blue is Blue – the World through –
Amber – Amber – Dew – Dew –
Seek – Friend – and see –
Heaven is shy of Earth – that's all –
Bashful Heaven – thy Lovers small –
Hide – too – from thee –

c. 1863   *1929*

287
(706)

Life, and Death, and Giants –
Such as These – are still –
Minor – Apparatus – Hopper of the Mill –
Beetle at the Candle –
Or a Fife's Fame –
Maintain – by Accident that they proclaim –

c. 1863   *1896*

288
(709)

Publication – is the Auction
Of the Mind of Man –
Poverty – be justifying
For so foul a thing

[176]

Possibly – but We – would rather
From Our Garret go
White – Unto the White Creator –
Than invest – Our Snow –

Thought belong to Him who gave it -
Then – to Him Who bear
Its Corporeal illustration – Sell
The Royal Air –

In the Parcel – Be the Merchant
Of the Heavenly Grace –
But reduce no Human Spirit
To Disgrace of Price –

c. 1863   1929

289
(711)

Strong Draughts of Their Refreshing Minds
To drink – enables Mine
Through Desert or the Wilderness
As bore it Sealed Wine –

To go elastic – Or as One
The Camel's trait – attained –
How powerful the Stimulus
Of an Hermetic Mind –

c. 1863   1929

290
(712)

Because I could not stop for Death –
He kindly stopped for me –

[177]

The Carriage held but just Ourselves –
And Immortality.

We slowly drove – He knew no haste
And I had put away
My labor and my leisure too,
For His Civility –

We passed the School, where Children strove
At Recess – in the Ring –
We passed the Fields of Gazing Grain –
We passed the Setting Sun –

Or rather – He passed Us –
The Dews drew quivering and chill –
For only Gossamer, my Gown –
My Tippet – only Tulle –

We paused before a House that seemed
A Swelling of the Ground –
The Roof was scarcely visible –
The Cornice – in the Ground –

Since then – 'tis Centuries – and yet
Feels shorter than the Day
I first surmised the Horses' Heads
Were toward Eternity –

:. 1863   1890

291
(713)
Fame of Myself, to justify,
All other Plaudit be
Superfluous – An Incense
Beyond Necessity –

[178]

Fame of Myself to lack – Although
My Name be else Supreme –
This were an Honor honorless –
A futile Diadem –

c. 1863   *1945*

292
(715)

The World – feels Dusty
When We stop to Die –
We want the Dew – then –
Honors – taste dry –

Flags – vex a Dying face –
But the least Fan
Stirred by a friend's Hand –
Cools – like the Rain –

Mine be the Ministry
When thy Thirst comes –
Dews of Thessaly, to fetch –
And Hybla Balms –

c. 1863   *1929*

293
(716)

The Day undressed – Herself –
Her Garter – was of Gold –
Her Petticoat – of Purple plain –
Her Dimities – as old

[179]

Exactly – as the World –
And yet the newest Star –
Enrolled upon the Hemisphere
Be wrinkled – much as Her –

Too near to God – to pray –
Too near to Heaven – to fear –
The Lady of the Occident
Retired without a care –

Her Candle so expire
The flickering be seen
On Ball of Mast in Bosporus –
And Dome – and Window Pane –

c. 1863   1935

294
(718)

I meant to find Her when I came –
Death – had the same design –
But the Success – was His – it seems –
And the Surrender – Mine –

I meant to tell Her how I longed
For just this single time –
But Death had told Her so the first –
And she had past, with Him –

To wander – now – is my Repose –
To rest – To rest would be
A privilege of Hurricane
To Memory – and Me.

c. 1863   1896

295
(719)

A South Wind – has a pathos
Of individual Voice –
As One detect on Landings
An Emigrant's address.

A Hint of Ports and Peoples –
And much not understood –
The fairer – for the farness –
And for the foreignhood.

c. 1863

194,

296
(721)

Behind Me – dips Eternity –
Before Me – Immortality –
Myself – the Term between –
Death but the Drift of Eastern Gray,
Dissolving into Dawn away,
Before the West begin –

'Tis Kingdoms – afterward – they say –
In perfect – pauseless Monarchy –
Whose Prince – is Son of None –
Himself – His Dateless Dynasty –
Himself – Himself diversify –
In Duplicate divine –

'Tis Miracle before Me – then –
'Tis Miracle behind – between –
A Crescent in the Sea –

With Midnight to the North of Her –
And Midnight to the South of Her –
And Maelstrom – in the Sky –

c. 1863   *1929*

297
(724)

It's easy to invent a Life –
God does it – every Day –
Creation – but the Gambol
Of His Authority –

It's easy to efface it –
The thrifty Deity
Could scarce afford Eternity
To Spontaneity –

The Perished Patterns murmur –
But His Perturbless Plan
Proceed – inserting Here – a Sun –
There – leaving out a Man –

e. 1863   *1929*

298
(725)

Where Thou art – that – is Home –
Cashmere – or Calvary – the same –
Degree – or Shame –
I scarce esteem Location's Name –
So I may Come –

What Thou dost – is Delight –
Bondage as Play – be sweet –

[182]

Imprisonment – Content –
And Sentence – Sacrament –
Just We two – meet –

Where Thou art not – is Woe –
Tho' Bands of Spices – row –
What Thou dost not – Despair –
Tho' Gabriel – praise me – Sir –

c. 1863   *1929*

299
(729)
Alter! When the Hills do –
Falter! When the Sun
Question if His Glory
Be the Perfect One –

Surfeit! When the Daffodil
Doth of the Dew –
Even as Herself – Sir –
I will – of You –

c. 1863   *1890*

300
(735)
Upon Concluded Lives
There's nothing cooler falls –
Than Life's sweet Calculations –
The mixing Bells and Palls

Makes Lacerating Tune –
To Ears the Dying Side –

[183]

'Tis Coronal – and Funeral –
Saluting – in the Road –

c. 1863   1945

301
(741)

Drama's Vitallest Expression is the Common Day
That arise and set about Us –
Other Tragedy

Perish in the Recitation –
This – the best enact
When the Audience is scattered
And the Boxes shut –

"Hamlet" to Himself were Hamlet –
Had not Shakespeare wrote –
Though the "Romeo" left no Record
Of his Juliet,

It were infinite enacted
In the Human Heart –
Only Theatre recorded
Owner cannot shut –

c. 1863   1929

302
(742)

Four Trees – upon a solitary Acre –
Without Design
Or Order, or Apparent Action –
Maintain –

The Sun – upon a Morning meets them –
The Wind –
No nearer Neighbor – have they –
But God –

The Acre gives them – Place –
They – Him – Attention of Passer by –
Of Shadow, or of Squirrel, haply –
Or Boy –

What Deed is Theirs unto the General Nature –
What Plan
They severally – retard – or further –
Unknown –

c. 1863   1945

303
(744)
Remorse – is Memory – awake –
Her Parties all astir –
A Presence of Departed Acts –
At window – and at Door –

Its Past – set down before the Soul
And lighted with a Match –
Perusal – to facilitate –
And help Belief to stretch –

Remorse is cureless – the Disease
Not even God – can heal –
For 'tis His institution – and
The Adequate of Hell –

c. 1863   1891

[185]

304
(745)

Renunciation – is a piercing Virtue –
The letting go
A Presence – for an Expectation –
Not now –
The putting out of Eyes –
Just Sunrise –
Lest Day –
Day's Great Progenitor –
Outvie
Renunciation – is the Choosing
Against itself –
Itself to justify
Unto itself –
When larger function –
Make that appear –
Smaller – that Covered Vision – Here –

c. 1863   1929

305
(749)

All but Death, can be Adjusted –
Dynasties repaired –
Systems – settled in their Sockets –
Citadels – dissolved –

Wastes of Lives – resown with Colors
By Succeeding Springs –
Death – unto itself – Exception –
Is exempt from Change –

c. 1863   1929

306
(750)

Growth of Man – like Growth of Nature –
Gravitates within –
Atmosphere, and Sun endorse it –
But it stir – alone –

Each – its difficult Ideal
Must achieve – Itself –
Through the solitary prowess
Of a Silent Life –

Effort – is the sole condition –
Patience of Itself –
Patience of opposing forces –
And intact Belief –

Looking on – is the Department
Of its Audience –
But Transaction – is assisted
By no Countenance –

c. 1863   *1929*

307
(754)

My Life had stood – a Loaded Gun –
In Corners – till a Day
The Owner passed – identified –
And carried Me away –

And now We roam in Sovereign Woods –
And now We hunt the Doe –
And every time I speak for Him –
The Mountains straight reply –

And do I smile, such cordial light
Upon the Valley glow –
It is as a Vesuvian face
Had let its pleasure through –

And when at Night – Our good Day done –
I guard My Master's Head –
'Tis better than the Eider-Duck's
Deep Pillow – to have shared –

To foe of His – I'm deadly foe –
None stir the second time –
On whom I lay a Yellow Eye –
Or an emphatic Thumb –

Though I than He – may longer live
He longer must – than I –
For I have but the power to kill,
Without – the power to die –

c. 1863   *1929*

308
(755)

No Bobolink – reverse His Singing
When the only Tree
Ever He minded occupying
By the Farmer be –

Clove to the Root –
His Spacious Future –
Best Horizon – gone –
Whose Music be His
Only Anodyne –
Brave Bobolink –

c. 1863   *1945*

309
(757)

The Mountains – grow unnoticed –
Their Purple figures rise
Without attempt – Exhaustion –
Assistance – or Applause –

In Their Eternal Faces
The Sun – with just delight
Looks long – and last – and golden –
For fellowship – at night –

c. 1863   *1929*

310
(761)

From Blank to Blank –
A Threadless Way
I pushed Mechanic feet –
To stop – or perish – or advance –
Alike indifferent –

If end I gained
It ends beyond
Indefinite disclosed –
I shut my eyes – and groped as well
'Twas lighter – to be Blind –

c. 1863   *1929*

311
(764)

Presentiment – is that long Shadow – on the Lawn –
Indicative that Suns go down –

[189]

The Notice to the startled Grass
That Darkness – is about to pass –

c. 1863   1890

312
(765)
You constituted Time –
I deemed Eternity
A Revelation of Yourself –
'Twas therefore Deity

The Absolute – removed
The Relative away –
That I unto Himself adjust
My slow idolatry –

c. 1863   1945

313
(766)
My Faith is larger than the Hills –
So when the Hills decay –
My Faith must take the Purple Wheel
To show the Sun the way –

'Tis first He steps upon the Vane –
And then – upon the Hill –
And then abroad the World He go
To do His Golden Will –

And if His Yellow feet should miss –
The Bird would not arise –
The Flowers would slumber on their Stems –
No Bells have Paradise –

[190]

How dare I, therefore, stint a faith
On which so vast depends –
Lest Firmament should fail for me –
The Rivet in the Bands

c. *1863*   *1929*

314
(769)

One and One – are One –
Two – be finished using –
Well enough for Schools –
But for Minor Choosing –

Life – just – Or Death –
Or the Everlasting –
More – would be too vast
For the Soul's Comprising –

c. *1863*   *1929*

315
(771)

None can experience stint
Who Bounty – have not known –
The fact of Famine – could not be
Except for Fact of Corn –

Want – is a meagre Art
Acquired by Reverse –
The Poverty that was not Wealth –
Cannot be Indigence.

c. *1863*   *1945*

[191]

316
(772)

The hallowing of Pain
Like hallowing of Heaven,
Obtains at a corporeal cost –
The Summit is not given

To Him who strives severe
At middle of the Hill –
But He who has achieved the Top –
All – is the price of All –

c. 1863   *1945*

317
(773)

Deprived of other Banquet,
I entertained Myself –
At first – a scant nutrition –
An insufficient Loaf –

But grown by slender addings
To so esteemed a size
'Tis sumptuous enough for me –
And almost to suffice

A Robin's famine able –
Red Pilgrim, He and I –
A Berry from our table
Reserve – for charity –

c. 1863   *1945*

318
(777)

The Loneliness One dare not sound –
And would as soon surmise
As in its Grave go plumbing
To ascertain the size –

The Loneliness whose worst alarm
Is lest itself should see –
And perish from before itself
For just a scrutiny –

The Horror not to be surveyed –
But skirted in the Dark –
With Consciousness suspended –
And Being under Lock –

I fear me this – is Loneliness –
The Maker of the soul
Its Caverns and its Corridors
Illuminate – or seal –

c. 1863   1945

319
(783)

The Birds begun at Four o'clock –
Their period for Dawn –
A Music numerous as space –
But neighboring as Noon –

I could not count their Force –
Their Voices did expend
As Brook by Brook bestows itself
To multiply the Pond.

[193]

Their Witnesses were not –
Except occasional man –
In homely industry arrayed –
To overtake the Morn –

Nor was it for applause –
That I could ascertain –
But independent Ecstasy
Of Deity and Men –

By Six, the Flood had done –
No Tumult there had been
Of Dressing, or Departure –
And yet the Band was gone –

The Sun engrossed the East –
The Day controlled the World –
The Miracle that introduced
Forgotten, as fulfilled.

c. *1863*   *1945*

320
(784)

Bereaved of all, I went abroad –
No less bereaved was I
Upon a New Peninsula –
The Grave preceded me –

Obtained my Lodgings, ere myself –
And when I sought my Bed –
The Grave it was reposed upon
The Pillow for my Head –

I waked to find it first awake –
I rose – It followed me –

[194]

I tried to drop it in the Crowd –
To lose it in the Sea –

In Cups of artificial Drowse
To steep its shape away –
The Grave – was finished – but the Spade
Remained in Memory –

c. 1863   1896

321
(789)
On a Columnar Self –
How ample to rely
In Tumult – or Extremity –
How good the Certainty

That Lever cannot pry –
And Wedge cannot divide
Conviction – That Granitic Base –
Though None be on our Side –

Suffice Us – for a Crowd –
Ourself – and Rectitude –
And that Assembly – not far off
From furthest Spirit – God –

c. 1863   1929

322
(790)
Nature – the Gentlest Mother is,
Impatient of no Child –

The feeblest – or the waywardest –
Her Admonition mild –

In Forest – and the Hill –
By Traveller – be heard –
Restraining Rampant Squirrel –
Or too impetuous Bird –

How fair Her Conversation –
A Summer Afternoon –
Her Household – Her Assembly –
And when the Sun go down –

Her Voice among the Aisles
Incite the timid prayer
Of the minutest Cricket –
The most unworthy Flower –

When all the Children sleep –
She turns as long away
As will suffice to light Her lamps –
Then bending from the Sky –

With infinite Affection –
And infiniter Care –
Her Golden finger on Her lip –
Wills Silence – Everywhere –

c. 1863   *1891*

323
(791)

God gave a Loaf to every Bird –
But just a Crumb – to Me –
I dare not eat it – tho' I starve –
My poignant luxury –

[196]

To own it – touch it –
Prove the feat – that made the Pellet mine –
Too happy – for my Sparrow's chance –
For Ampler Coveting –

It might be Famine – all around –
I could not miss an Ear –
Such Plenty smiles upon my Board –
My Garner shows so fair –

I wonder how the Rich – may feel –
An Indiaman – An Earl –
I deem that I – with but a Crumb –
Am Sovereign of them all –

c. 1863   1891

324
(792)
Through the strait pass of suffering –
The Martyrs – even – trod.
Their feet – upon Temptation –
Their faces – upon God –

A stately – shriven – Company –
Convulsion – playing round –
Harmless – as streaks of Meteor –
Upon a Planet's Bond –

Their faith – the everlasting troth –
Their Expectation – fair –
The Needle – to the North Degree –
Wades – so – thro' polar Air!

c. 1863   1891

[197]

Grief is a Mouse –
And chooses Wainscot in the Breast
For His Shy House –
And baffles quest –

Grief is a Thief – quick startled –
Pricks His Ear – report to hear
Of that Vast Dark –
That swept His Being – back –

Grief is a Juggler – boldest at the Play –
Lest if He flinch – the eye that way
Pounce on His Bruises – One – say – or Three –
Grief is a Gourmand – spare His luxury –

Best Grief is Tongueless – before He'll tell –
Burn Him in the Public Square –
His Ashes – will
Possibly – if they refuse – How then know –
Since a Rack couldn't coax a syllable – now.

c. 1863   *1945*

325
(797)

By my Window have I for Scenery
Just a Sea – with a Stem –
If the Bird and the Farmer – deem it a "Pine" –
The Opinion will serve – for them –

It has no Port, nor a "Line" – but the Jays –
That split their route to the Sky –
Or a Squirrel, whose giddy Peninsula
May be easier reached – this way –

For Inlands – the Earth is the under side –
And the upper side – is the Sun –
And its Commerce – if Commerce it have –
Of Spice – I infer from the Odors borne –

Of its Voice – to affirm – when the Wind is within –
Can the Dumb – define the Divine?
The Definition of Melody – is –
That Definition is none –

It – suggests to our Faith –
They – suggest to our Sight –
When the latter – is put away
I shall meet with Conviction I somewhere met
That Immortality –

Was the Pine at my Window a "Fellow
Of the Royal" Infinity?
Apprehensions – are God's introductions –
To be hallowed – accordingly –

c. 1863   1929

327
(798)

She staked her Feathers – Gained an Arc –
Debated – Rose again –
This time – beyond the estimate
Of Envy, or of Men –

And now, among Circumference –
Her steady Boat be seen –
At home – among the Billows – As
The Bough where she was born –

c. 1863   1935

328
(800)

Two – were immortal twice –
The privilege of few –
Eternity – obtained – in Time –
Reversed Divinity –

That our ignoble Eyes
The quality conceive
Of Paradise superlative –
Through their Comparative.

c. *1863*   *1945*

329
(802)

Time feels so vast that were it not
For an Eternity –
I fear me this Circumference
Engross my Finity –

To His exclusion, who prepare
By Processes of Size
For the Stupendous Vision
Of His diameters –

                                                                                   1935

330
(808)

So set its Sun in Thee
What Day be dark to me –
What Distance – far –

So I the Ships may see
That touch – how seldomly –
Thy Shore?

c. *1864*

1914

331
(812)
A Light exists in Spring
Not present on the Year
At any other period –
When March is scarcely here

A Color stands abroad
On Solitary Fields
That Science cannot overtake
But Human Nature feels.

It waits upon the Lawn,
It shows the furthest Tree
Upon the furthest Slope you know
It almost speaks to you.

Then as Horizons step
Or Noons report away
Without the Formula of sound
It passes and we stay –

A quality of loss
Affecting our Content
As Trade had suddenly encroached
Upon a Sacrament.

c. *1864*

1896

332
(813)

This quiet Dust was Gentlemen and Ladies
And Lads and Girls –
Was laughter and ability and Sighing
And Frocks and Curls.

This Passive Place a Summer's nimble mansion
Where Bloom and Bees
Exists an Oriental Circuit
Then cease, like these –

c. 1864   1914

333
(815)

The Luxury to apprehend
The Luxury 'twould be
To look at Thee a single time
An Epicure of Me

In whatsoever Presence makes
Till for a further Food
I scarcely recollect to starve
So first am I supplied –

The Luxury to meditate
The Luxury it was
To banquet on thy Countenance
A Sumptuousness bestows

On plainer Days, whose Table far
As Certainty can see
Is laden with a single Crumb
The Consciousness of Thee.

c. 1864   1914

334
(816)

A Death blow is a Life blow to Some
Who till they died, did not alive become –
Who had they lived, had died but when
They died, Vitality begun.

c. 1864   1891

335
(817)

Given in Marriage unto Thee
Oh thou Celestial Host –
Bride of the Father and the Son
Bride of the Holy Ghost.

Other Betrothal shall dissolve –
Wedlock of Will, decay –
Only the Keeper of this Ring
Conquer Mortality –

c. 1864   1896

336
(820)

All Circumstances are the Frame
In which His Face is set –
All Latitudes exist for His
Sufficient Continont

The Light His Action, and the Dark
The Leisure of His Will –

In Him Existence serve or set
A Force illegible.

c. 1864   1914

337
(821)

Away from Home are some and I –
An Emigrant to be
In a Metropolis of Homes
Is easy, possibly –

The Habit of a Foreign Sky
We – difficult – acquire
As Children, who remain in Face
The more their Feet retire.

c. 1864   1894

338
(822)

This Consciousness that is aware
Of Neighbors and the Sun
Will be the one aware of Death
And that itself alone

Is traversing the interval
Experience between
And most profound experiment
Appointed unto Men –

How adequate unto itself
Its properties shall be

Itself unto itself and none
Shall make discovery.

Adventure most unto itself
The Soul condemned to be –
Attended by a single Hound
Its own identity.

c. 1864   1945

339
(824)
The Wind begun to knead the Grass –
As Women do a Dough –
He flung a Hand full at the Plain –
A Hand full at the Sky –
The Leaves unhooked themselves from Trees –
And started all abroad –
The Dust did scoop itself like Hands –
And throw away the Road –
The Wagons quickened on the Street –
The Thunders gossiped low –
The Lightning showed a Yellow Head –
And then a livid Toe –
The Birds put up the Bars to Nests –
The Cattle flung to Barns –
Then came one drop of Giant Rain –
And then, as if the Hands
That held the Dams – had parted hold –
The Waters Wrecked the Sky –
But overlooked my Father's House –
Just Quartering a Tree –

first version
c. 1864   1955

[205]

The Wind begun to rock the Grass
With threatening Tunes and low –
He threw a Menace at the Earth –
A Menace at the Sky.

The Leaves unhooked themselves from Trees –
And started all abroad
The Dust did scoop itself like Hands
And threw away the Road.

The Wagons quickened on the Streets
The Thunder hurried slow –
The Lightning showed a Yellow Beak
And then a livid Claw.

The Birds put up the Bars to Nests –
The Cattle fled to Barns –
There came one drop of Giant Rain
And then as if the Hands

That held the Dams had parted hold
The Waters Wrecked the Sky,
But overlooked my Father's House –
Just quartering a Tree –

second version
c. 1864   *1891*

340
(827)
The Only News I know
Is Bulletins all Day
From Immortality.

The Only Shows I see –
Tomorrow and Today –
Perchance Eternity –

The Only One I meet
Is God – The Only Street –
Existence – This traversed

If Other News there be –
Or Admirabler Show –
I'll tell it You –

c. 1864   1929

341
(829)

Ample make this Bed –
Make this Bed with Awe –
In it wait till Judgment break
Excellent and Fair.

Be its Mattress straight –
Be its Pillow round –
Let no Sunrise' yellow noise
Interrupt this Ground –

c. 1864   1891

342
(831)

Dying! To be afraid of thee
One must to thine Artillery
Have left exposed a Friend –

Than thine old Arrow is a Shot
Delivered straighter to the Heart
The leaving Love behind.

Not for itself, the Dust is shy,
But, enemy, Beloved be
Thy Batteries divorce.
Fight sternly in a Dying eye
Two Armies, Love and Certainty
And Love and the Reverse.

c. *1864*   *1945*

343
(834)

Before He comes we weigh the Time!
'Tis Heavy and 'tis Light.
When He depart, an Emptiness
Is the prevailing Freight.

c. *1864*   *1894*

344
(835)

Nature and God – I neither knew
Yet Both so well knew me
They startled, like Executors
Of My identity.

Yet Neither told – that I could learn –
My Secret as secure
As Herschel's private interest
Or Mercury's affair –

c. *1864*   *1894*

345
(836)

Truth – is as old as God –
His Twin identity
And will endure as long as He
A Co-Eternity –

And perish on the Day
Himself is borne away
From Mansion of the Universe
A lifeless Deity.

c. 1864   *1894*

346
(854)

Banish Air from Air –
Divide Light if you dare –
They'll meet
While Cubes in a Drop
Or Pellets of Shape
Fit
Films cannot annul
Odors return whole
Force Flame
And with a Blonde push
Over your impotence
Flits Steam.

c. 1864   *1945*

347
(855)

To own the Art within the Soul
The Soul to entertain

[209]

With Silence as a Company
And Festival maintain

Is an unfurnished Circumstance
Possession is to One
As an Estate perpetual
Or a reduceless Mine.

c. *1864*   *1945*

348
(856)

There is a finished feeling
Experienced at Graves –
A leisure of the Future –
A Wilderness of Size.

By Death's bold Exhibition
Preciser what we are
And the Eternal function
Enabled to infer.

c. *1864*   *1945*

349
(857)

Uncertain lease – develops lustre
On Time
Uncertain Grasp, appreciation
Of Sum –

The shorter Fate – is oftener the chiefest
Because

[210]

Inheritors upon a tenure
Prize –

c. 1864   1945

350
(860)
Absence disembodies – so does Death
Hiding individuals from the Earth
Superstition helps, as well as love –
Tenderness decreases as we prove –

c. 1864   1945

351
(861)
Split the Lark – and you'll find the Music –
Bulb after Bulb, in Silver rolled –
Scantily dealt to the Summer Morning
Saved for your Ear when Lutes be old.

Loose the Flood – you shall find it patent –
Gush after Gush, reserved for you –
Scarlet Experiment! Sceptic Thomas!
Now, do you doubt that your Bird was true?

c. 1864   1896

352
(862)
Light is sufficient to itself –
If Others want to see

It can be had on Window Panes
Some Hours in the Day.

But not for Compensation –
It holds as large a Glow
To Squirrel in the Himmaleh
Precisely, as to you.

c. 1864   *1945*

353
(864)

The Robin for the Crumb
Returns no syllable
But long records the Lady's name
In Silver Chronicle.

c. 1864   *1945*

354
(871)

The Sun and Moon must make their haste –
The Stars express around
For in the Zones of Paradise
The Lord alone is burned –

His Eye, it is the East and West –
The North and South when He
Do concentrate His Countenance
Like Glow Worms, flee away –

Oh Poor and Far –
Oh Hindered Eye

That hunted for the Day –
The Lord a Candle entertains
Entirely for Thee –

c. *1864*   *1945*

355
(872)

As the Starved Maelstrom laps the Navies
As the Vulture teased
Forces the Broods in lonely Valleys
As the Tiger eased

By but a Crumb of Blood, fasts Scarlet
Till he meet a Man
Dainty adorned with Veins and Tissues
And partakes – his Tongue

Cooled by the Morsel for a moment
Grows a fiercer thing
Till he esteem his Dates and Cocoa
A Nutrition mean

I, of a finer Famine
Deem my Supper dry
For but a Berry of Domingo
And a Torrid Eye.

c. *1864*   *1945*

356
(875)

I stepped from Plank to Plank
A slow and cautious way

The Stars about my Head I felt
About my Feet the Sea.

I knew not but the next
Would be my final inch –
This gave me that precarious Gait
Some call Experience.

c. 1864   *1896*

357
(883)
The Poets light but Lamps –
Themselves – go out –
The Wicks they stimulate –
If vital Light

Inhere as do the Suns –
Each Age a Lens
Disseminating their
Circumference –

c. 1864   *1945*

358
(884)
An Everywhere of Silver
With Ropes of Sand
To keep it from effacing
The Track called Land.

1864   *1891*

359
(887)

We outgrow love, like other things
And put it in the Drawer –
Till it an Antique fashion shows –
Like Costumes Grandsires wore.

c. 1864   *1896*

360
(889)

Crisis is a Hair
Toward which the forces creep
Past which forces retrograde
If it come in sleep

To suspend the Breath
Is the most we can
Ignorant is it Life or Death
Nicely balancing.

Let an instant push
Or an Atom press
Or a Circle hesitate
In Circumference

It – may jolt the Hand
That adjusts the Hair
That secures Eternity
From presenting – Here –

c. 1864   *1945*

[215]

361
(893)

Drab Habitation of Whom?
Tabernacle or Tomb –
Or Dome of Worm –
Or Porch of Gnome –
Or some Elf's Catacomb?

c. 1864   *1896*

362
(894)

Of Consciousness, her awful Mate
The Soul cannot be rid –
As easy the secreting her
Behind the Eyes of God.

The deepest hid is sighted first
And scant to Him the Crowd –
What triple Lenses burn upon
The Escapade from God –

c. 1864   *1945*

363
(896)

Of Silken Speech and Specious Shoe
A Traitor is the Bee
His service to the newest Grace
Present continually

His Suit a chance
His Troth a Term
Protracted as the Breeze

[216]

Continual Ban propoundeth He
Continual Divorce.

c. 1864   *1945*

364
(900)

What did They do since I saw Them?
Were They industrious?
So many questions to put Them
Have I the eagerness

That could I snatch Their Faces
That could Their lips reply
Not till the last was answered
Should They start for the Sky.

Not if Their Party were waiting,
Not if to talk with Me
Were to Them now, Homesickness
After Eternity.

Not if the Just suspect me
And offer a Reward
Would I restore my Booty
To that Bold Person, God –

c. 1864   *1945*

365
(906)

The Admirations – and Contempts – of time –
Show justest – through an Open Tomb –

The Dying – as it were a Height
Reorganizes Estimate
And what We saw not
We distinguish clear –
And mostly – see not
What We saw before –

'Tis Compound Vision –
Light – enabling Light –
The Finite – furnished
With the Infinite –
Convex – and Concave Witness –
Back – toward Time –
And forward –
Toward the God of Him –

c. 1864   1929

366
(907)

Till Death – is narrow Loving –
The scantest Heart extant
Will hold you till your privilege
Of Finiteness – be spent –

But He whose loss procures you
Such Destitution that
Your Life too abject for itself
Thenceforward imitate –

Until – Resemblance perfect –
Yourself, for His pursuit
Delight of Nature – abdicate –
Exhibit Love – somewhat –

c. 1864   1929

367
(910)

Experience is the Angled Road
Preferred against the Mind
By – Paradox – the Mind itself –
Presuming it to lead

Quite Opposite – How Complicate
The Discipline of Man –
Compelling Him to Choose Himself
His Preappointed Pain –

c. 1864   *1929*

368
(911)

Too little way the House must lie
From every Human Heart
That holds in undisputed Lease
A white inhabitant –

Too narrow is the Right between –
Too imminent the chance –
Each Consciousness must emigrate
And lose its neighbor once –

c. 1864   *1935*

369
(913)

And this of all my Hopes
This, is the silent end

Bountiful colored, my Morning rose
Early and sere, its end

Never Bud from a Stem
Stepped with so gay a Foot
Never a Worm so confident
Bored at so brave a Root

c. 1864   *1929*

370
(917)

Love – is anterior to Life –
Posterior – to Death –
Initial of Creation, and
The Exponent of Earth –

c. 1864   *1896*

371
(918)

Only a Shrine, but Mine –
I made the Taper shine –
Madonna dim, to whom all Feet may come,
Regard a Nun –

Thou knowest every Woe –
Needless to tell thee – so –
But can'st thou do
The Grace next to it – heal?
That looks a harder skill to us –
Still – just as easy, if it be thy Will

To thee – Grant me –
Thou knowest, though, so Why tell thee?

c. 1864   1929

372
(919)

If I can stop one Heart from breaking
I shall not live in vain
If I can ease one Life the Aching
Or cool one Pain

Or help one fainting Robin
Unto his Nest again
I shall not live in Vain.

c. 1864   1890

373
(922)

Those who have been in the Grave the longest –
Those who begin Today –
Equally perish from our Practise –
Death is the other way –

Foot of the Bold did least attempt it –
It – is the White Exploit –
Once to achieve, annuls the power
Once to communicate –

c. 1864   1945

374
(928)

The Heart has narrow Banks
It measures like the Sea
In mighty – unremitting Bass
And Blue Monotony

Till Hurricane bisect
And as itself discerns
Its insufficient Area
The Heart convulsive learns

That Calm is but a Wall
Of unattempted Gauze
An instant's Push demolishes
A Questioning – dissolves.

r. 1864   1945

375
(943)

A Coffin – is a small Domain,
Yet able to contain
A Citizen of Paradise
In its diminished Plane.

A Grave – is a restricted Breadth –
Yet ampler than the Sun –
And all the Seas He populates
And Lands He looks upon

To Him who on its small Repose
Bestows a single Friend –
Circumference without Relief –
Or Estimate – or End –

c. 1864   1945

376
(946)

It is an honorable Thought
And makes One lift One's Hat
As One met sudden Gentlefolk
Upon a daily Street

That We've immortal Place
Though Pyramids decay
And Kingdoms, like the Orchard
Flit Russetly away

c. 1864   *1896*

377
(949)

Under the Light, yet under,
Under the Grass and the Dirt,
Under the Beetle's Cellar
Under the Clover's Root,

Further than Arm could stretch
Were it Giant long,
Further than Sunshine could
Were the Day Year long,

Over the Light, yet over,
Over the Arc of the Bird –
Over the Comet's chimney –
Over the Cubit's Head,

Further than Guess can gallop
Further than Riddle ride –
Oh for a Disc to the Distance
Between Ourselves and the Dead!

c. 1864   *1945*

378
(959)

A loss of something ever felt I –
The first that I could recollect
Bereft I was – of what I knew not
Too young that any should suspect

A Mourner walked among the children
I notwithstanding went about
As one bemoaning a Dominion
Itself the only Prince cast out –

Elder, Today, a session wiser
And fainter, too, as Wiseness is –
I find myself still softly searching
For my Delinquent Palaces –

And a Suspicion, like a Finger
Touches my Forehead now and then
That I am looking oppositely
For the site of the Kingdom of Heaven –

c. 1864   *1945*

379
(960)

As plan for Noon and plan for Night
So differ Life and Death
In positive Prospective –
The Foot upon the Earth

At Distance, and Achievement, strains,
The Foot upon the Grave
Makes effort at conclusion
Assisted faint of Love.

c. 1864   *1945*

[224]

380
(963)

A nearness to Tremendousness –
An Agony procures –
Affliction ranges Boundlessness –
Vicinity to Laws

Contentment's quiet Suburb –
Affliction cannot stay
In Acres – Its Location
Is Illocality –

c. 1864   1935

381
(964)

"Unto Me?" I do not know you –
Where may be your House?

"I am Jesus – Late of Judea –
Now – of Paradise" –

Wagons – have you – to convey me?
This is far from Thence –

"Arms of Mine – sufficient Phaeton –
Trust Omnipotence" –

I am spotted – "I am Pardon" –
I am small – "The Least
Is esteemed in Heaven the Chiefest –
Occupy my House" –

c. 1864   1929

382
(969)

He who in Himself believes –
Fraud cannot presume –
Faith is Constancy's Result –
And assumes – from Home –

Cannot perish, though it fail
Every second time –
But defaced Vicariously –
For Some Other Shame –

c. 1864   1945

383
(970)

Color – Caste – Denomination –
These – are Time's Affair –
Death's diviner Classifying
Does not know they are –

As in sleep – All Hue forgotten –
Tenets – put behind –
Death's large – Democratic fingers
Rub away the Brand –

If Circassian – He is careless –
If He put away
Chrysalis of Blonde – or Umber –
Equal Butterfly –

They emerge from His Obscuring –
What Death – knows so well –
Our minuter intuitions –
Deem unplausible –

c. 1864   1929

384
(974)
The Soul's distinct connection
With immortality
Is best disclosed by Danger
Or quick Calamity –

As Lightning on a Landscape
Exhibits Sheets of Place –
Not yet suspected – but for Flash –
And Click – and Suddenness.

c. 1864   1925

385
(975)
The Mountain sat upon the Plain
In his tremendous Chair –
His observation omnifold,
His inquest, everywhere –

The Seasons played around his knees
Like Children round a sire –
Grandfather of the Days is He
Of Dawn, the Ancestor –

c. 1864   1890

386
(976)
Death is a Dialogue between
The Spirit and the Dust.
"Dissolve" says Death – The Spirit "Sir
I have another Trust" –

[227]

Death doubts it – Argues from the Ground –
The Spirit turns away
Just laying off for evidence
An Overcoat of Clay.

c. 1864   1890

387
(982)

No Other can reduce
Our mortal Consequence
Like the remembering it be nought
A Period from hence
But Contemplation for
Contemporaneous Nought
Our Single Competition
Jehovah's Estimate.

c. 1865   1914

388
(985)

The Missing All – prevented Me
From missing minor Things.
If nothing larger than a World's
Departure from a Hinge –
Or Sun's extinction, be observed –
'Twas not so large that I
Could lift my Forehead from my work
For Curiosity.

c. 1865   1914

A narrow Fellow in the Grass
Occasionally rides –
You may have met Him – did you not
His notice sudden is –

The Grass divides as with a Comb –
A spotted shaft is seen –
And then it closes at your feet
And opens further on –

He likes a Boggy Acre
A Floor too cool for Corn –
Yet when a Boy, and Barefoot –
I more than once at Noon

Have passed, I thought, a Whip lash
Unbraiding in the Sun
When stóoping to secure it
It wrinkled, and was gone –

Several of Nature's People
I know, and they know me –
I feel for them a transport
Of cordiality –

But never met this Fellow
Attended, or alone
Without a tighter breathing
And Zero at the Bone –

c. *1865*   *1866*

The Leaves like Women interchange
Exclusive Confidence –

[229]

Somewhat of nods and somewhat
Portentous inference.

The Parties in both cases
Enjoining secrecy –
Inviolable compact
To notoriety.

c. 1865   *1891*

391
(988)

The Definition of Beauty is
That Definition is none –
Of Heaven, easing Analysis,
Since Heaven and He are one.

c. 1865   *1924*

392
(997)

Crumbling is not an instant's Act
A fundamental pause
Dilapidation's processes
Are organized Decays.

'Tis first a Cobweb on the Soul
A Cuticle of Dust
A Borer in the Axis
An Elemental Rust –

Ruin is formal – Devil's work
Consecutive and slow –
Fail in an instant, no man did
Slipping – is Crash's law.

c. 1865   *1945*

393
(999)

Superfluous were the Sun
When Excellence be dead
He were superfluous every Day
For every Day be said

That syllable whose Faith
Just saves it from Despair
And whose "I'll meet You" hesitates
If Love inquire "Where"?

Upon His dateless Fame
Our Periods may lie
As Stars that drop anonymous
From an abundant sky.

c. 1865   *1896*

394
(1005)

Bind me – I still can sing –
Banish – my mandolin
Strikes true within –

Slay – and my Soul shall rise
Chanting to Paradise –
Still thine.

c. 1865   *1945*

395
(1013)

Too scanty 'twas to die for you,
The merest Greek could that.

⌈ 231 ⌉

The living, Sweet, is costlier –
I offer even that –

The Dying, is a trifle, past,
But living, this include
The dying multifold – without
The Respite to be dead.

c. 1865   1945

396
(1017)

To die – without the Dying
And live – without the Life
This is the hardest Miracle
Propounded to Belief.

c. 1865   1945

397
(1024)

So large my Will
The little that I may
Embarrasses
Like gentle infamy –

Affront to Him
For whom the Whole were small
Affront to me
Who knew His Meed of all.

Earth at the best
Is but a scanty Toy –

[232]

Bought, carried Home
To Immortality.

It looks so small
We chiefly wonder then
At our Conceit
In purchasing.

c. *1865*   *1945*

398
(1026)

The Dying need but little, Dear,
A Glass of Water's all,
A Flower's unobtrusive Face
To punctuate the Wall,

A Fan, perhaps, a Friend's Regret
And Certainty that one
No color in the Rainbow
Perceive, when you are gone.

c. *1865*   *1896*

399
(1035)

Bee! I'm expecting you!
Was saying Yesterday
To Somebody you know
That you were due –

The Frogs got Home last Week –
Are settled, and at work –

Birds, mostly back –
The Clover warm and thick –

You'll get my Letter by
The seventeenth; Reply
Or better, be with me –
Yours, Fly.

c. *1865*   *1945*

400
(1039)

I heard, as if I had no Ear
Until a Vital Word
Came all the way from Life to me
And then I knew I heard.

I saw, as if my Eye were on
Another, till a Thing
And now I know 'twas Light, because
It fitted them, came in.

I dwelt, as if Myself were out,
My Body but within
Until a Might detected me
And set my kernel in.

And Spirit turned unto the Dust
"Old Friend, thou knowest me,"
And Time went out to tell the News
And met Eternity.

c. *1865*   *1945*

401
(1046)

I've dropped my Brain – My Soul is numb –
The Veins that used to run
Stop palsied – 'tis Paralysis
Done perfecter on stone

Vitality is Carved and cool.
My nerve in Marble lies –
A Breathing Woman
Yesterday – Endowed with Paradise.

Not dumb – I had a sort that moved –
A Sense that smote and stirred –
Instincts for Dance – a caper part –
An Aptitude for Bird –

Who wrought Carrara in me
And chiselled all my tune
Were it a Witchcraft – were it Death –
I've still a chance to strain

To Being, somewhere – Motion – Breath –
Though Centuries beyond,
And every limit a Decade –
I'll shiver, satisfied.

c. 1865   1945

402
(1051)

I cannot meet the Spring unmoved –
I feel the old desire –
A Hurry with a lingering, mixed,
A Warrant to be fair –

A Competition in my sense
With something hid in Her –
And as she vanishes, Remorse
I saw no more of Her.

c. 1865   *1945*

403
(1052)

I never saw a Moor –
I never saw the Sea –
Yet know I how the Heather looks
And what a Billow be.

I never spoke with God
Nor visited in Heaven –
Yet certain am I of the spot
As if the Checks were given –

c. 1865   *1890*

404
(1053)

It was a quiet way –
He asked if I was his –
I made no answer of the Tongue
But answer of the Eyes –
And then He bore me on
Before this mortal noise
With swiftness, as of Chariots
And distance, as of Wheels.

[236]

This World did drop away
As Acres from the feet
Of one that leaneth from Balloon
Upon an Ether street.
The Gulf behind was not,
The Continents were new –
Eternity it was before
Eternity was due.
No Seasons were to us –
It was not Night nor Morn –
But Sunrise stopped upon the place
And fastened it in Dawn.

c. *1865*   *1929*

405
(1055)
The Soul should always stand ajar
That if the Heaven inquire
He will not be obliged to wait
Or shy of troubling Her

Depart, before the Host have slid
The Bolt unto the Door –
To search for the accomplished Guest,
Her Visitor, no more –

c. *1865*   *1896*

406
(1056)
There is a Zone whose even Years
No Solstice interrupt –

[237]

Whose Sun constructs perpetual Noon
Whose perfect Seasons wait –

Whose Summer set in Summer, till
The Centuries of June
And Centuries of August cease
And Consciousness – is Noon.

c. 1865   *1945*

407
(1060)

Air has no Residence, no Neighbor,
No Ear, no Door,
No Apprehension of Another
Oh, Happy Air!

Ethereal Guest at e'en an Outcast's Pillow –
Essential Host, in Life's faint, wailing Inn,
Later than Light thy Consciousness accost me
Till it depart, persuading Mine –

c. 1865   *1945*

408
(1065)

Let down the Bars, Oh Death –
The tired Flocks come in
Whose bleating ceases to repeat
Whose wandering is done –

Thine is the stillest night
Thine the securest Fold

[238]

Too near Thou art for seeking Thee
Too tender, to be told.

c. 1865   1891

409
(1067)

Except the smaller size
No lives are round –
These – hurry to a sphere
And show and end –
The larger – slower grow
And later hang –
The Summers of Hesperides
Are long.

c. 1866   189

410
(1068)

Further in Summer than the Birds
Pathetic from the Grass
A minor Nation celebrates
Its unobtrusive Mass.

No Ordinance be seen
So gradual the Grace
A pensive Custom it becomes
Enlarging Loneliness.

Antiquest felt at Noon
When August burning low

Arise this spectral Canticle
Repose to typify

Remit as yet no Grace
No Furrow on the Glow
Yet a Druidic Difference
Enhances Nature now

c. 1866   *1891*

411
(1071)

Perception of an object costs
Precise the Object's loss –
Perception in itself a Gain
Replying to its Price –
The Object Absolute – is nought –
Perception sets it fair
And then upbraids a Perfectness
That situates so far –

c. 1866   *1914*

412
(1072)

Title divine – is mine!
The Wife – without the Sign!
Acute Degree – conferred on me –
Empress of Calvary!
Royal – all but the Crown!
Betrothed – without the swoon
God sends us Women –
When you – hold – Garnet to Garnet –

Gold – to Gold –
Born – Bridalled – Shrouded –
In a Day –
Tri Victory
"My Husband" – women say –
Stroking the Melody –
Is *this* – the way?

c. 1862   1924

413
(1073)

Experiment to me
Is every one I meet
If it contain a Kernel?
The Figure of a Nut

Presents upon a Tree
Equally plausibly,
But Meat within, is requisite
To Squirrels, and to Me.

c. 1865   1891

414
(1075)

The Sky is low – the Clouds are mean.
A Travelling Flake of Snow
Across a Barn or through a Rut
Debates if it will go –

A Narrow Wind complains all Day
How some one treated him

Nature, like Us is sometimes caught
Without her Diadem.

c. 1866   1890

415
(1078)

The Bustle in a House
The Morning after Death
Is solemnest of industries
Enacted upon Earth –

The Sweeping up the Heart
And putting Love away
We shall not want to use again
Until Eternity.

c. 1866   1890

416
(1081)

Superiority to Fate
Is difficult to gain
'Tis not conferred of Any
But possible to earn

A pittance at a time
Until to Her surprise
The Soul with strict economy
Subsist till Paradise.

c 1866   1896

417
(1082)

Revolution is the Pod
Systems rattle from
When the Winds of Will are stirred
Excellent is Bloom

But except its Russet Base
Every Summer be
The Entomber of itself,
So of Liberty –

Left inactive on the Stalk
All its Purple fled
Revolution shakes it for
Test if it be dead.

c. 1866   1929

418
(1083)

We learn in the Retreating
How vast an one
Was recently among us –
A Perished Sun

Endear in the departure
How doubly more
Than all the Golden presence
It was – before –

c. 1866   1896

At Half past Three, a single Bird
Unto a silent Sky
Propounded but a single term
Of cautious melody.

At Half past Four, Experiment
Had subjugated test
And lo, Her silver Principle
Supplanted all the rest.

At Half past Seven, Element
Nor Implement, be seen –
And Place was where the Presence was
Circumference between.

c. 1866   *1891*

420
(1097)

Dew – is the Freshet in the Grass –
'Tis many a tiny Mill
Turns unperceived beneath our feet
And Artisan lies still –

We spy the Forests and the Hills
The Tents to Nature's Show
Mistake the Outside for the in
And mention what we saw.

Could Commentators on the Sign
Of Nature's Caravan
Obtain "Admission" as a Child
Some Wednesday Afternoon.

c. 1866   *1914*

421

(1099)

My Cocoon tightens – Colors tease –
I'm feeling for the Air –
A dim capacity for Wings
Demeans the Dress I wear –

A power of Butterfly must be –
The Aptitude to fly
Meadows of Majesty implies
And easy Sweeps of Sky –

So I must baffle at the Hint
And cipher at the Sign
And make much blunder, if at last
I take the clue divine –

c. 1866   1890

422

(1100)

The last Night that She lived
It was a Common Night
Except the Dying – this to Us
Made Nature different

We noticed smallest things –
Things overlooked before
By this great light upon our Minds
Italicized – as 'twere.

As We went out and in
Between Her final Room
And Rooms where Those to be alive
Tomorrow were, a Blame

[245]

That Others could exist
While She must finish quite
A Jealousy for Her arose
So nearly infinite –

We waited while She passed –
It was a narrow time –
Too jostled were Our Souls to speak
At length the notice came.

She mentioned, and forgot –
Then lightly as a Reed
Bent to the Water, struggled scarce –
Consented, and was dead –

And We – We placed the Hair –
And drew the Head erect –
And then an awful leisure was
Belief to regulate –

c. 1866   1890

423
(1104)

The Crickets sang
And set the Sun
And Workmen finished one by one
Their Seam the Day upon.

The low Grass loaded with the Dew
The Twilight stood, as Strangers do
With Hat in Hand, polite and new
To stay as if, or go.

A Vastness, as a Neighbor, came,
A Wisdom, without Face, or Name.

[246]

A Peace, as Hemispheres at Home
And so the Night became.

c. 1866   1896

424
(1123)
A great Hope fell
You heard no noise
The Ruin was within
Oh cunning wreck that told no tale
And let no Witness in

The mind was built for mighty Freight
For dread occasion planned
How often foundering at Sea
Ostensibly, on Land

A not admitting of the wound
Until it grew so wide
That all my Life had entered it
And there were troughs beside

A closing of the simple lid
That opened to the sun
Until the tender Carpenter
Perpetual nail it down –

c. 1868   1945

425
(1125)
Oh Sumptuous moment
Slower go
That I may gloat on thee –

'Twill never be the same to starve
Now I abundance see –

Which was to famish, then or now –
The difference of Day
Ask him unto the Gallows led –
With morning in the sky –

c. 1868   1945

426
(1126)

Shall I take thee, the Poet said
To the propounded word?
Be stationed with the Candidates
Till I have finer tried –

The Poet searched Philology
And when about to ring
For the suspended Candidate
There came unsummoned in –

That portion of the Vision
The Word applied to fill
Not unto nomination
The Cherubim reveal –

c. 1868   1945

427
(1129)

Tell all the Truth but tell it slant –
Success in Circuit lies

Too bright for our infirm Delight
The Truth's superb surprise
As Lightning to the Children eased
With explanation kind
The Truth must dazzle gradually
Or every man be blind –

c. 1868   *1945*

428
(1134)
The Wind took up the Northern Things
And piled them in the south –
Then gave the East unto the West
And opening his mouth

The four Divisions of the Earth
Did make as to devour
While everything to corners slunk
Behind the awful power –

The Wind – unto his Chambers went
And nature ventured out –
Her subjects scattered into place
Her systems ranged about

Again the smoke from Dwellings rose
The Day abroad was heard –
How intimate, a Tempest past
The Transport of the Bird –

c. 1868   *1945*

[249]

429
(1136)

The Frost of Death was on the Pane –
"Secure your Flower" said he.
Like Sailors fighting with a Leak
We fought Mortality.

Our passive Flower we held to Sea –
To Mountain – To the Sun –
Yet even on his Scarlet shelf
To crawl the Frost begun –

We pried him back
Ourselves we wedged
Himself and her between,
Yet easy as the narrow Snake
He forked his way along

Till all her helpless beauty bent
And then our wrath begun –
We hunted him to his Ravine
We chased him to his Den –

We hated Death and hated Life
And nowhere was to go –
Than Sea and continent there is
A larger – it is Woe –

c. 1869

1945

430
(1137)

The duties of the Wind are few,
To cast the ships, at Sea,
Establish March, the Floods escort,
And usher Liberty.

⌈ 250 ⌉

The pleasures of the Wind are broad,
To dwell Extent among,
Remain, or wander,
Speculate, or Forests entertain.

The kinsmen of the Wind are Peaks
Azof – the Equinox,
Also with Bird and Asteroid
A bowing intercourse.

The limitations of the Wind
Do he exist, or die,
Too wise he seems for Wakelessness,
However, know not I.

c. 1869   *1945*

431
(1138)

A Spider sewed at Night
Without a Light
Upon an Arc of White.

If Ruff it was of Dame
Or Shroud of Gnome
Himself himself inform.

Of Immortality
His Strategy
Was Physiognomy.

c. 1869   *1891*

432
(1142)

The Props assist the House
Until the House is built

[251]

And then the Props withdraw
And adequate, erect,
The House support itself
And cease to recollect
The Auger and the Carpenter –
Just such a retrospect
Hath the perfected Life –
A past of Plank and Nail
And slowness – then the Scaffolds drop
Affirming it a Soul.

1863   1914

433
(1144)

Ourselves we do inter with sweet derision.
The channel of the dust who once achieves
Invalidates the balm of that religion
That doubts as fervently as it believes.

1 869?   1894

434
(1147)

After a hundred years
Nobody knows the Place
Agony that enacted there
Motionless as Peace

Weeds triumphant ranged
Strangers strolled and spelled
At the lone Orthography
Of the Elder Dead

Winds of Summer Fields
Recollect the way –
Instinct picking up the Key
Dropped by memory –

c. 1869   *1891*

435
(1155)

Distance – is not the Realm of Fox
Nor by Relay of Bird
Abated – Distance is
Until thyself, Beloved.

c. 1870   *1914*

436
(1158)

Best Witchcraft is Geometry
To the magician's mind –
His ordinary acts are feats
To thinking of mankind.

c. 1870   *1932*

437
(1170)

Nature affects to be sedate
Upon occasion, grand

⌈ 253 ⌉

But let our observation shut
Her practices extend

To Necromancy and the Trades
Remote to understand
Behold our spacious Citizen
Unto a Juggler turned –

c. 1870   *1945*

438
(1171)

On the World you colored
Morning painted rose –
Idle his Vermilion
Aimless crept the Glows
Over Realms of Orchards
I the Day before
Conquered with the Robin –
Misery, how fair
Till your wrinkled Finger
Shored the sun away
Midnight's awful Pattern
In the Goods of Day –

c. 1870   *1945*

439
(1176)

We never know how high we are
Till we are asked to rise
And then if we are true to plan
Our statures touch the skies –

[254]

The Heroism we recite
Would be a normal thing
Did not ourselves the Cubits warp
For fear to be a King –

c. 1870   1896

440
(1177)

A prompt – executive Bird is the Jay –
Bold as a Bailiff's Hymn –
Brittle and Brief in quality –
Warrant in every line –

Sitting a Bough like a Brigadier
Confident and straight –
Much is the mien of him in March
As a Magistrate –

c. 1865   1914

441
(1186)

Too few the mornings be,
Too scant the nights.
No lodging can be had
For the delights
That come to earth to stay,
But no apartment find
And ride away.

1871   1894

442
(1193)

All men for Honor hardest work
But are not known to earn –
Paid after they have ceased to work
In Infamy or Urn –

c. 1871   1945

443
(1197)

I should not dare to be so sad
So many Years again –
A Load is first impossible
When we have put it down –

The Superhuman then withdraws
And we who never saw
The Giant at the other side
Begin to perish now.

1871   1929

444
(1206)

The Show is not the Show
But they that go –
Menagerie to me
My Neighbor be –
Fair Play –
Both went to see –

c. 1872   1891

445

(1207)

He preached upon "Breadth" till it argued him narrow –
The Broad are too broad to define
And of "Truth" until it proclaimed him a Liar –
The Truth never flaunted a Sign –

Simplicity fled from his counterfeit presence
As Gold the Pyrites would shun –
What confusion would cover the innocent Jesus
To meet so enabled a Man!

c. 1872   1891

446

(1209)

To disappear enhances –
The Man that runs away
Is tinctured for an instant
With Immortality

But yesterday a Vagrant –
Today in Memory lain
With superstitious value
We tamper with "Again"

But "Never" far as Honor
Withdraws the Worthless thing
And impotent to cherish
We hasten to adorn –

Of Death the sternest function
That just as we discern
The Excellence defies us –
Securest gathered then

The Fruit perverse to plucking,
But leaning to the Sight
With the ecstatic limit
Of unobtained Delight –

c. 1872   1894

447
(1212)

A word is dead
When it is said,
Some say.
I say it just
Begins to live
That day.

1872?   1894

448
(1213)

We like March.
His Shoes are Purple –
He is new and high –
Makes he Mud for Dog and Peddler,
Makes he Forests dry.
Knows the Adder Tongue his coming
And presents her Spot –
Stands the Sun so close and mighty
That our Minds are hot.

News is he of all the others –
Bold it were to die

[258]

With the Blue Birds exercising
On his British Sky.

version of 1872   *1955*

We like March – his shoes are Purple.
He is new and high –
Makes he Mud for Dog and Peddler –
Makes he Forests Dry –
Knows the Adder's Tongue his coming
And begets her spot –
Stands the Sun so close and mighty –
That our Minds are hot.
News is he of all the others –
Bold it were to die
With the Blue Birds buccaneering
On his British sky –

version of 1878   *1896*

449
(1214)

We introduce ourselves
To Planets and to Flowers
But with ourselves
Have etiquettes
Embarrassments
And awes

c. 1872   *1945*

150
(1222)

'The Riddle we can guess
We speedily despise –

[259]

Not anything is stale so long
As Yesterday's surprise –

c. 1870   1945

451
(1225)

Its Hour with itself
The Spirit never shows.
What Terror would enthrall the Street
Could Countenance disclose

The Subterranean Freight
The Cellars of the Soul –
Thank God the loudest Place he made
Is licensed to be still.

c. 1872   1929

452
(1226)

The Popular Heart is a Cannon first –
Subsequent a Drum –
Bells for an Auxiliary
And an Afterward of Rum –

Not a Tomorrow to know its name
Nor a Past to stare –
Ditches for Realms and a Trip to Jail
For a Souvenir –

c. 1872   1929

453
(1227)

My Triumph lasted till the Drums
Had left the Dead alone
And then I dropped my Victory
And chastened stole along
To where the finished Faces
Conclusion turned on me
And then I hated Glory
And wished myself were They.

What is to be is best descried
When it has also been –
Could Prospect taste of Retrospect
The tyrannies of Men
Were Tenderer – diviner
The Transitive toward.
A Bayonet's contrition
Is nothing to the Dead.

c. 1872   1935

454
(1230)

It came at last but prompter Death
Had occupied the House –
His pallid Furniture arranged
And his metallic Peace –

Oh faithful Frost that kept the Date
Had Love as punctual been
Delight had aggrandized the Gate
And blocked the coming in.

c. 1872   1945

455
(1231)

Somewhere upon the general Earth
Itself exist Today –
The Magic passive but extant
That consecrated me –

Indifferent Seasons doubtless play
Where I for right to be –
Would pay each Atom that I am
But Immortality –

Reserving that but just to prove
Another Date of Thee –
Oh God of Width, do not for us
Curtail Eternity!

c. 1872   1945

456
(1232)

The Clover's simple Fame
Remembered of the Cow –
Is better than enameled Realms
Of notability.
Renown perceives itself
And that degrades the Flower –
The Daisy that has looked behind
Has compromised its power –

c. 1872   1945

457
(1241)

The Lilac is an ancient shrub
But ancienter than that

The Firmamental Lilac
Upon the Hill tonight –
The Sun subsiding on his Course
Bequeaths this final Plant
To Contemplation – not to Touch –
The Flower of Occident.
Of one Corolla is the West –
The Calyx is the Earth –
The Capsules burnished Seeds the Stars
The Scientist of Faith
His research has but just begun –
Above his synthesis
The Flora unimpeachable
To Time's Analysis –
"Eye hath not seen" may possibly
Be current with the Blind
But let not Revelation
By theses be detained –

c. 1872   1945

458
(1243)

Safe Despair it is that raves –
Agony is frugal.
Puts itself severe away
For its own perusal.

Garrisoned no Soul can be
In the Front of Trouble –
Love is one, not aggregate –
Nor is Dying double –

c. 1873   1914

459
(1244)

The Butterfly's Assumption Gown
In Chrysoprase Apartments hung
This afternoon put on –

How condescending to descend
And be of Buttercups the friend
In a New England Town –

c. 1873   1890

460
(1246)

The Butterfly in honored Dust
Assuredly will lie
But none will pass the Catacomb
So chastened as the Fly –

c. 1873   1915

461
(1254)

Elijah's Wagon knew no thill
Was innocent of Wheel
Elijah's horses as unique
As was his vehicle –

Elijah's journey to portray
Expire with him the skill
Who justified Elijah
In feats inscrutable –

c. 1873   1914

462
(1255)
Longing is like the Seed
That wrestles in the Ground,
Believing if it intercede
It shall at length be found.

The Hour, and the Clime –
Each Circumstance unknown,
What Constancy must be achieved
Before it see the Sun!

c. 1873   1929

463
(1256)
Not any higher stands the Grave
For Heroes than for Men –
Not any nearer for the Child
Than numb Three Score and Ten –

This latest Leisure equal lulls
The Beggar and his Queen
Propitiate this Democrat
A Summer's Afternoon –

c. 1873   1896

464
(1260)
Because that you are going
And never coming back

[265]

And I, however absolute,
May overlook your Track –

Because that Death is final,
However first it be,
This instant be suspended
Above Mortality –

Significance that each has lived
The other to detect
Discovery not God himself
Could now annihilate

Eternity, Presumption
The instant I perceive
That you, who were Existence
Yourself forgot to live –

The "Life that is" will then have been
A thing I never knew –
As Paradise fictitious
Until the Realm of you –

The "Life that is to be," to me,
A Residence too plain
Unless in my Redeemer's Face
I recognize your own –

Of Immortality who doubts
He may exchange with me
Curtailed by your obscuring Face
Of everything but He –

Of Heaven and Hell I also yield
The Right to reprehend
To whoso would commute this Face
For his less priceless Friend.

If "God is Love" as he admits
We think that he must be
Because he is a "jealous God"
He tells us certainly

If "All is possible with" him
As he besides concedes
He will refund us finally
Our confiscated Gods –

c. *1873*   *1930*

465
(1261)

A Word dropped careless on a Page
May stimulate an eye
When folded in perpetual seam
The Wrinkled Maker lie

Infection in the sentence breeds
We may inhale Despair
At distances of Centuries
From the Malaria –

c. *1873*   *1947*

466
(1263)

There is no Frigate like a Book
To take us Lands away
Nor any Coursers like a Page
Of prancing Poetry –

This Traverse may the poorest take
Without oppress of Toll –
How frugal is the Chariot
That bears the Human soul.

c. 1873   1894

467
(1265)

The most triumphant Bird I ever knew or met
Embarked upon a twig today
And till Dominion set
I famish to behold so eminent a sight
And sang for nothing scrutable
But intimate Delight.
Retired, and resumed his transitive Estate –
To what delicious Accident
Does finest Glory fit!

c. .873   1894

468
(1269)

I worked for chaff and earning Wheat
Was haughty and betrayed.
What right had Fields to arbitrate
In matters ratified?

I tasted Wheat and hated Chaff
And thanked the ample friend –
Wisdom is more becoming viewed
At distance than at hand.

c. 1873   1896

469
(1271)

September's Baccalaureate
A combination is
Of Crickets – Crows – and Retrospects
And a dissembling Breeze

That hints without assuming –
An Innuendo sear
That makes the Heart put up its Fun
And turn Philosopher.

c. 1873   *1892*

470
(1276)

'Twas later when the summer went
Than when the Cricket came –
And yet we knew that gentle Clock
Meant nought but Going Home –
'Twas sooner when the Cricket went
Than when the Winter came
Yet that pathetic Pendulum
Keeps esoteric Time.

c. 1873   *1890*

471
(1282)

Art thou the thing I wanted?
Begone – my Tooth has grown –
Affront a minor palate
Thou could'st not goad so long –

[269]

I tell thee while I waited –
The mystery of Food
Increased till I abjured it
Subsisting now like God –

c. 1873   1945

472
(1286)

I thought that nature was enough
Till Human nature came
But that the other did absorb
As Parallax a Flame –

Of Human nature just aware
There added the Divine
Brief struggle for capacity
The power to contain

Is always as the contents
But give a Giant room
And you will lodge a Giant
And not a smaller man

c. 1873   1945

473
(1295)

Two Lengths has every Day –
Its absolute extent
And Area superior
By Hope or Horror lent –

Eternity will be
Velocity or Pause
At Fundamental Signals
From Fundamental Laws.

To die is not to go –
On Doom's consummate Chart
No Territory new is staked –
Remain thou as thou art.

c. 1874   1914

474
(1298)

The Mushroom is the Elf of Plants –
At Evening, it is not –
At Morning, in a Truffled Hut
It stop upon a Spot

As if it tarried always
And yet its whole Career
Is shorter than a Snake's Delay
And fleeter than a Tare –

'Tis Vegetation's Juggler –
The Germ of Alibi –
Doth like a Bubble antedate
And like a Bubble, hie –

I feel as if the Grass was pleased
To have it intermit –
This surreptitious scion
Of Summer's circumspect.

Had Nature any supple Face
Or could she one contemn –

Had Nature an Apostate –
That Mushroom – it is Him!

c. 1874   1891

475
(1304)

Not with a Club, the Heart is broken
Nor with a Stone –
A Whip so small you could not see it
I've known

To lash the Magic Creature
Till it fell,
Yet that Whip's Name
Too noble then to tell.

Magnanimous as Bird
By Boy descried –
Singing unto the Stone
Of which it died –

Shame need not crouch
In such an Earth as Ours –
Shame – stand erect –
The Universe is yours.

c. 1874   1896

476
(1307)

That short – potential stir
That each can make but once –

That Bustle so illustrious
'Tis almost Consequence –

Is the éclat of Death –
Oh, thou unknown Renown
That not a Beggar would accept
Had he the power to spurn –

c. 1874   1890

477
(1320)

Dear March – Come in –
How glad I am –
I hoped for you before –
Put down your Hat –
You must have walked –
How out of Breath you are –
Dear March, how are you, and the Rest –
Did you leave Nature well –
Oh March, Come right up stairs with me –
I have so much to tell –

I got your Letter, and the Birds –
The Maples never knew that you were coming – till I called
I declare – how Red their Faces grew –
But March, forgive me – and
All those Hills you left for me to Hue –
There was no Purple suitable –
You took it all with you –

Who knocks? That April.
Lock the Door –
I will not be pursued –
He stayed away a Year to call

[273]

When I am occupied –
But trifles look so trivial
As soon as you have come

That Blame is just as dear as Praise
And Praise as mere as Blame –

c. 1874   1896

478
(1332)
Pink – small – and punctual –
Aromatic – low –
Covert – in April –
Candid – in May –
Dear to the Moss –
Known to the Knoll –
Next to the Robin
In every human Soul –
Bold little Beauty
Bedecked with thee
Nature forswears
Antiquity –

c. 1875   1890

479
(1333)
A little Madness in the Spring
Is wholesome even for the King,
But God be with the Clown –

[274]

Who ponders this tremendous scene –
This whole Experiment of Green –
As if it were his own!

·. 1875   *1914*

480
(1334)

How soft this Prison is
How sweet these sullen bars
No Despot but the King of Down
Invented this repose

Of Fate if this is All
Has he no added Realm
A Dungeon but a Kinsman is
Incarceration – Home.

c. 1875   *1951*

481
(1335)

Let me not mar that perfect Dream
By an Auroral stain
But so adjust my daily Night
That it will come again.

Not when we know, the Power accosts –
The Garment of Surprise
Was all our timid Mother wore
At Home – in Paradise.

c. 1875   *1947*

482
(1338)

What tenements of clover
Are fitting for the bee,
What edifices azure
For butterflies and me –
What residences nimble
Arise and evanesce
Without a rhythmic rumor
Or an assaulting guess.

1875?   *1894*

483
(1339)

A Bee his burnished Carriage
Drove boldly to a Rose –
Combinedly alighting –
Himself – his Carriage was –
The Rose received his visit
With frank tranquillity
Withholding not a Crescent
To his Cupidity –
Their Moment consummated –
Remained for him – to flee –
Remained for her – of rapture
But the humility.

c. 1875   *1945*

484
(1340)

A Rat surrendered here
A brief career of Cheer
And Fraud and Fear.

[276]

Of Ignominy's due
Let all addicted to
Beware.

The most obliging Trap
Its tendency to snap
Cannot resist –

Temptation is the Friend
Repugnantly resigned
At last.

c. 1875   1945

485
(1343)

A single Clover Plank
Was all that saved a Bee
A Bee I personally knew
From sinking in the sky –

'Twixt Firmament above
And Firmament below
The Billows of Circumference
Were sweeping him away –

The idly swaying Plank
Responsible to nought
A sudden Freight of Wind assumed
And Bumble Bee was not –

This harrowing event
Transpiring in the Grass
Did not so much as wring from him
A wandering "Alas" –

c. 1875   1945

486
(1353)

The last of Summer is Delight –
Deterred by Retrospect.
'Tis Ecstasy's revealed Review –
Enchantment's Syndicate.

To meet it – nameless as it is –
Without celestial Mail –
Audacious as without a Knock
To walk within the Veil.

c. 1876   1929

487
(1354)

The Heart is the Capital of the Mind –
The Mind is a single State –
The Heart and the Mind together make
A single Continent –

One – is the Population –
Numerous enough –
This ecstatic Nation
Seek – it is Yourself.

c. 1876   1929

488
(1355)

The Mind lives on the Heart
Like any Parasite –
If that is full of Meat
The Mind is fat.

[278]

But if the Heart omit
Emaciate the Wit –
The Aliment of it
So absolute.

c. 1876   1932

489
(1356)

The Rat is the concisest Tenant.
He pays no Rent.
Repudiates the Obligation –
On Schemes intent

Balking our Wit
To sound or circumvent –
Hate cannot harm
A Foe so reticent –
Neither Decree prohibit him –
Lawful as Equilibrium.

c. 1876   1891

490
(1357)

"Faithful to the end" Amended
From the Heavenly Clause –
Constancy with a Proviso
Constancy abhors –

"Crowns of Life" are servile Prizes
To the stately Heart,

Given for the Giving, solely,
No Emolument.

version I
c. *1876*

1932

"Faithful to the end" Amended
From the Heavenly clause –
Lucrative indeed the offer
But the Heart withdraws –

"I will give" the base Proviso –
Spare Your "Crown of Life" –
Those it fits, too fair to wear it –
Try it on Yourself –

version II
c. *1876*

1945

491
(1371)

How fits his Umber Coat
The Tailor of the Nut?
Combined without a seam
Like Raiment of a Dream –

Who spun the Auburn Cloth?
Computed how the girth?
The Chestnut aged grows
In those primeval Clothes –

We know that we are wise –
Accomplished in Surprise –
Yet by this Countryman –
This nature – how undone!

c. *1876*

1945

492
(1374)

A Saucer holds a Cup
In sordid human Life
But in a Squirrel's estimate
A Saucer hold a Loaf.

A Table of a Tree
Demands the little King
And every Breeze that run along
His Dining Room do swing.

His Cutlery – he keeps
Within his Russet Lips –
To see it flashing when he dines
Do Birmingham eclipse –

Convicted – could we be
Of our Minutiae
The smallest Citizen that flies
Is heartier than we –

c. 1876   *1945*

493
(1379)

His Mansion in the Pool
The Frog forsakes –
He rises on a Log
And statements makes –
His Auditors two Worlds
Deducting me –
The Orator of April
Is hoarse Today –

His Mittens at his Feet
No Hand hath he –
His eloquence a Bubble
As Fame should be –
Applaud him to discover
To your chagrin
Demosthenes has vanished
In Waters Green –

c. 1876

1945

494
(1393)

Lay this Laurel on the One
Too intrinsic for Renown –
Laurel – veil your deathless tree –
Him you chasten, that is He!

c. 1877

1891

495
(1396)

She laid her docile Crescent down
And this confiding Stone
Still states to Dates that have forgot
The News that she is gone –

So constant to its stolid trust,
The Shaft that never knew –
It shames the Constancy that fled
Before its emblem flew –

c. 1877

1896

496
(1397)

It sounded as if the Streets were running
And then – the Streets stood still –
Eclipse – was all we could see at the Window
And Awe – was all we could feel.

By and by – the boldest stole out of his Covert
To see if Time was there –
Nature was in an Opal Apron,
Mixing fresher Air.

c. 1877   *1891*

497
(1398)

I have no Life but this –
To lead it here –
Nor any Death – but lest
Dispelled from there –

Nor tie to Earths to come –
Nor Action new –
Except through this extent –
The Realm of you –

c. 1877   *1891*

498
(1400)

What mystery pervades a well!
That water lives so far –

[283]

A neighbor from another world
Residing in a jar

Whose limit none have ever seen,
But just his lid of glass –
Like looking every time you please
In an abyss's face!

The grass does not appear afraid,
I often wonder he
Can stand so close and look so bold
At what is awe to me.

Related somehow they may be,
The sedge stands next the sea –
Where he is floorless
And does no timidity betray

But nature is a stranger yet;
The ones that cite her most
Have never passed her haunted house,
Nor simplified her ghost.

To pity those that know her not
Is helped by the regret
That those who know her, know her less
The nearer her they get.

1877?   1896

499
(1404)

March is the Month of Expectation.
The things we do not know –
The Persons of prognostication
Are coming now –

[284]

We try to show becoming firmness –
But pompous Joy
Betrays us, as his first Betrothal
Betrays a Boy.

c. 1877   *1914*

500
(1405)

Bees are Black, with Gilt Surcingles –
Buccaneers of Buzz.
Ride abroad in ostentation
And subsist on Fuzz.

Fuzz ordained – not Fuzz contingent –
Marrows of the Hill.
Jugs – a Universe's fracture
Could not jar or spill.

c. 1877   *1945*

501
(1407)

A Field of Stubble, lying sere
Beneath the second Sun –
Its Toils to Brindled People thrust –
Its Triumphs – to the Bin –
Accosted by a timid Bird
Irresolute of Alms
Is often seen – but seldom felt,
On our New England Farms –

c. 1877   *1932*

502
(1433)

How brittle are the Piers
On which our Faith doth tread –
No Bridge below doth totter so –
Yet none hath such a Crowd.

It is as old as God –
Indeed – 'twas built by him –
He sent his Son to test the Plank,
And he pronounced it firm.

c. 1878   1894

503
(1437)

A Dew sufficed itself –
And satisfied a Leaf
And felt "how vast a destiny" –
"How trivial is Life!"

The Sun went out to work –
The Day went out to play
And not again that Dew be seen
By Physiognomy

Whether by Day Abducted
Or emptied by the Sun
Into the Sea in passing
Eternally unknown

Attested to this Day
That awful Tragedy
By Transport's instability
And Doom's celerity.

c. 1878   1896

504
(1445)

Death is the supple Suitor
That wins at last —
It is a stealthy Wooing
Conducted first
By pallid innuendoes
And dim approach
But brave at last with Bugles
And a bisected Coach
It bears away in triumph
To Troth unknown
And Kindred as responsive
As Porcelain.

c. 1878   1945

505
(1452)

Your thoughts don't have words every day
They come a single time
Like signal esoteric sips
Of the communion Wine
Which while you taste so native seems
So easy so to be
You cannot comprehend its price
Nor its infrequency

c. 1878   1945

506
(1454)

Those not live yet
Who doubt to live again —

[287]

"Again" is of a twice
But this – is one –
The Ship beneath the Draw
Aground – is he?
Death – so – the Hyphen of the Sea –
Deep is the Schedule
Of the Disk to be –
Costumeless Consciousness –
That is he –

c. 1879   1932

507
(1461)

"Heavenly Father" – take to thee
The supreme iniquity
Fashioned by thy candid Hand
In a moment contraband –
Though to trust us – seem to us
More respectful – "We are Dust" –
We apologize to thee
For thine own Duplicity –

c. 1879   1914

508
(1463)

A Route of Evanescence
With a revolving Wheel –
A Resonance of Emerald –
A Rush of Cochineal –
And every Blossom on the Bush
Adjusts its tumbled Head –

[288]

The mail from Tunis, probably,
An easy Morning's Ride –

c. 1879 1891

509
(1465)

Before you thought of Spring
Except as a Surmise
You see – God bless his suddenness –
A Fellow in the Skies
Of independent Hues
A little weather worn
Inspiriting habiliments
Of Indigo and Brown –
With specimens of Song
As if for you to choose –
Discretion in the interval
With gay delays he goes
To some superior Tree
Without a single Leaf
And shouts for joy to Nobody
But his seraphic self –

c. 1871 1891

510
(1466)

One of the ones that Midas touched
Who failed to touch us all
Was that confiding Prodigal
The reeling Oriole –

So drunk he disavows it
With badinage divine –
So dazzling we mistake him
For an alighting Mine –

A Pleader – a Dissembler –
An Epicure – a Thief –
Betimes an Oratorio –
An Ecstasy in chief –

The Jesuit of Orchards
He cheats as he enchants
Of an entire Attar
For his decamping wants –

The splendor of a Burmah
The Meteor of Birds,
Departing like a Pageant
Of Ballads and of Bards –

I never thought that Jason sought
For any Golden Fleece
But then I am a rural man
With thoughts that make for Peace –

But if there were a Jason,
Tradition bear with me
Behold his lost Aggrandizement
Upon the Apple Tree –

c. *1879*   *1891*

511
(1474)
Estranged from Beauty – none can be –
For Beauty is Infinity –

[290]

And power to be finite ceased
Before Identity was leased.

c. 1879   1945

512
(1475)

Fame is the one that does not stay –
Its occupant must die
Or out of sight of estimate
Ascend incessantly –
Or be that most insolvent thing
A Lightning in the Germ –
Electrical the embryo
But we demand the Flame

c. 1879   1945

513
(1479)

The Devil – had he fidelity
Would be the best friend –
Because he has ability –
But Devils cannot mend –
Perfidy is the virtue
That would but he resign
The Devil – without question
Were thoroughly divine

c. 1879   1914

514
(1483)

The Robin is a Gabriel
In humble circumstances –
His Dress denotes him socially,
Of Transport's Working Classes –
He has the punctuality
Of the New England Farmer –
The same oblique integrity,
A Vista vastly warmer –

A small but sturdy Residence,
A self denying Household,
The Guests of Perspicacity
Are all that cross his Threshold –
As covert as a Fugitive,
Cajoling Consternation
By Ditties to the Enemy
And Sylvan Punctuation –

c. 1880   1894

515
(1485)

Love is done when Love's begun,
Sages say,
But have Sages known?
Truth adjourn your Boon
Without Day.

c. 1880   1894

516
(1487)

The Savior must have been
A docile Gentleman –
To come so far so cold a Day
For little Fellowmen –

The Road to Bethlehem
Since He and I were Boys
Was leveled, but for that 'twould be
A rugged billion Miles –

c. 1880   1915

517
(1501)

Its little Ether Hood
Doth sit upon its Head –
The millinery supple
Of the sagacious God –

Till when it slip away
A nothing at a time –
And Dandelion's Drama
Expires in a stem.

c. 1880   1945

518
(1509)

Mine Enemy is growing old –
I have at last Revenge –

The Palate of the Hate departs –
If any would avenge

Let him be quick – the Viand flits –
It is a faded Meat –
Anger as soon as fed is dead –
'Tis starving makes it fat –

c. 1881 1891

519
(1510)

How happy is the little Stone
That rambles in the Road alone,
And doesn't care about Careers
And Exigencies never fears –
Whose Coat of elemental Brown
A passing Universe put on,
And independent as the Sun
Associates or glows alone,
Fulfilling absolute Decree
In casual simplicity –

c. 1881 1891

520
(1514)

An Antiquated Tree
Is cherished of the Crow
Because that Junior Foliage is disrespectful now
To venerable Birds
Whose Corporation Coat

Would decorate Oblivion's
Remotest Consulate.

c. *1881*   *1945*

521
(1519)
The Dandelion's pallid tube
Astonishes the Grass,
And Winter instantly becomes
An infinite Alas –
The tube uplifts a signal Bud
And then a shouting Flower, --
The Proclamation of the Suns
That sepulture is o'er.

c. *1881*   *1894*

522
(1522)
His little Hearse like Figure
Unto itself a Dirge
To a delusive Lilac
The vanity divulge
Of Industry and Morals
And every righteous thing
For the divine Perdition
Of Idleness and Spring

c. *1881*   *1915*

523
(1540)

As imperceptibly as Grief
The Summer lapsed away –
Too imperceptible at last
To seem like Perfidy –
A Quietness distilled
As Twilight long begun,
Or Nature spending with herself
Sequestered Afternoon –
The Dusk drew earlier in –
The Morning foreign shone –
A courteous, yet harrowing Grace,
As Guest, that would be gone –
And thus, without a Wing
Or service of a Keel
Our Summer made her light escape
Into the Beautiful.

c. 1865   1891

524
(1542)

Come show thy Durham Breast
To her who loves thee best,
Delicious Robin –
And if it be not me
At least within my Tree
Do the avowing –
Thy Nuptial so minute
Perhaps is more astute
Than vaster suing –

[296]

For so to soar away
Is our propensity
The Day ensuing –

c. 1882   1947

525
(1545)

The Bible is an antique Volume –
Written by faded Men
At the suggestion of Holy Spectres –
Subjects – Bethlehem –
Eden – the ancient Homestead –
Satan – the Brigadier –
Judas – the Great Defaulter –
David – the Troubadour –
Sin – a distinguished Precipice
Others must resist –
Boys that "believe" are very lonesome –
Other Boys are "lost" –
Had but the Tale a warbling Teller –
All the Boys would come –
Orpheus' Sermon captivated –
It did not condemn –

c. 1882   1924

526
(1550)

The pattern of the sun
Can fit but him alone
For sheen must have a Disk
To be a sun –

c. 1882   1945

527
(1551)

Those – dying then,
Knew where they went –
They went to God's Right Hand –
That Hand is amputated now
And God cannot be found –

The abdication of Belief
Makes the Behavior small –
Better an ignis fatuus
Than no illume at all –

c. 1882   1945

528
(1556)

Image of Light, Adieu –
Thanks for the interview –
So long – so short –
Preceptor of the whole –
Coeval Cardinal –
Impart – Depart –

c. 1882   1945

529
(1561)

No Brigadier throughout the Year
So civic as the Jay –
A Neighbor and a Warrior too
With shrill felicity

Pursuing Winds that censure us
A February Day,
The Brother of the Universe
Was never blown away –
The Snow and he are intimate –
I've often seen them play
When Heaven looked upon us all
With such severity
I felt apology were due
To an insulted sky
Whose pompous frown was Nutriment
To their Temerity –
The Pillow of this daring Head
Is pungent Evergreens –
His Larder – terse and Militant –
Unknown – refreshing things –
His Character – a Tonic –
His Future – a Dispute –
Unfair an Immortality
That leaves this Neighbor out –

c. 1883   189

530
(1564)
Pass to thy Rendezvous of Light,
Pangless except for us –
Who slowly ford the Mystery
Which thou hast leaped across!

c. 1883   1924

531
(1567)

The Heart has many Doors –
I can but knock –
For any sweet "Come in"
Impelled to hark –
Not saddened by repulse,
Repast to me
That somewhere, there exists,
Supremacy –

c. 1883   *1955*

532
(1570)

Forever honored be the Tree
Whose Apple Winterworn
Enticed to Breakfast from the Sky
Two Gabriels Yestermorn.

They registered in Nature's Book
As Robins – Sire and Son –
But Angels have that modest way
To screen them from Renown.

·. 1883   *1914*

533
(1575)

The Bat is dun, with wrinkled Wings –
Like fallow Article –
And not a song pervade his Lips –
Or none perceptible.

[300]

His small Umbrella quaintly halved
Describing in the Air
An Arc alike inscrutable
Elate Philosopher.

Deputed from what Firmament –
Of what Astute Abode –
Empowered with what Malignity
Auspiciously withheld –

To his adroit Creator
Ascribe no less the praise –
Beneficent, believe me,
His Eccentricities –

c. 1876   1891

534
(1581)

The farthest Thunder that I heard
Was nearer than the Sky
And rumbles still, though torrid Noons
Have lain their missiles by –
The Lightning that preceded it
Struck no one but myself –
But I would not exchange the Bolt
For all the rest of Life –
Indebtedness to Oxygen
The Happy may repay,
But not the obligation
To Electricity –
It founds the Homes and decks the Days
And every clamor bright

[301]

Is but the gleam concomitant
Of that waylaying Light –
The Thought is quiet as a Flake –
A Crash without a Sound,
How Life's reverberation
Its Explanation found –

c. 1883   *1932*

535
(1585)

The Bird her punctual music brings
And lays it in its place –
Its place is in the Human Heart
And in the Heavenly Grace –
What respite from her thrilling toil
Did Beauty ever take –
But Work might be electric Rest
To those that Magic make –

1883   *1955*

536
(1587)

He ate and drank the precious Words –
His Spirit grew robust –
He knew no more that he was poor,
Nor that his frame was Dust –

He danced along the dingy Days
And this Bequest of Wings

[302]

Was but a Book – What Liberty
A loosened spirit brings –

1883   *189ι*

537
(1593)

There came a Wind like a Bugle –
It quivered through the Grass
And a Green Chill upon the Heat
So ominous did pass
We barred the Windows and the Doors
As from an Emerald Ghost –
The Doom's electric Moccasin
That very instant passed –
On a strange Mob of panting Trees
And Fences fled away
And Rivers where the Houses ran
Those looked that lived – that Day –
The Bell within the steeple wild
The flying tidings told –
How much can come
And much can go,
And yet abide the World!

c. 1883   *1891*

538
(1594)

Immured in Heaven!
What a Cell!
Let every Bondage be,

[303]

Thou sweetest of the Universe,
Like that which ravished thee!

c. *1883*

1914

539
(1599)

Though the great Waters sleep,
That they are still the Deep,
We cannot doubt –
No vacillating God
Ignited this Abode
To put it out –

c. *1884*

1894

540
(1601)

Of God we ask one favor,
That we may be forgiven –
For what, he is presumed to know –
The Crime, from us, is hidden –
Immured the whole of Life
Within a magic Prison
We reprimand the Happiness
That too competes with Heaven.

:. *1884*

1894

541
(1612)

The Auctioneer of Parting
His "Going, going, gone"

Shouts even from the Crucifix,
And brings his Hammer down –
He only sells the Wilderness,
The prices of Despair
Range from a single human Heart
To Two – not any more –

c. 1884   1945

542
(1624)

Apparently with no surprise
To any happy Flower
The Frost beheads it at its play –
In accidental power –
The blonde Assassin passes on –
The Sun proceeds unmoved
To measure off another Day
For an Approving God.

c. 1884   1890

543
(1625)

Back from the cordial Grave I drag thee
He shall not take thy Hand
Nor put his spacious arm around thee
That none can understand

c. 1884   1915

544
(1627)

The pedigree of Honey
Does not concern the Bee,
Nor lineage of Ecstasy
Delay the Butterfly
On spangled journeys to the peak
Of some perceiveless thing –
The right of way to Tripoli
A more essential thing.

version I
c. 1884   1945

The Pedigree of Honey
Does not concern the Bee –
A Clover, any time, to him,
Is Aristocracy –

version II
c. 1884   1890

545
(1635)

The Jay his Castanet has struck
Put on your muff for Winter
The Tippet that ignores his voice
Is impudent to nature

Of Swarthy Days he is the close
His Lotus is a chestnut
The Cricket drops a sable line
No more from yours at present

c. 1884   1945

546
(1651)

A Word made Flesh is seldom
And tremblingly partook
Nor then perhaps reported
But have I not mistook
Each one of us has tasted
With ecstasies of stealth
The very food debated
To our specific strength –

A Word that breathes distinctly
Has not the power to die
Cohesive as the Spirit
It may expire if He –
"Made Flesh and dwelt among us"
Could condescension be
Like this consent of Language
This loved Philology.

? *1955*

547
(1654)

Beauty crowds me till I die
Beauty mercy have on me
But if I expire today
Let it be in sight of thee –

? *1914*

548
(1657)

Eden is that old-fashioned House
We dwell in every day

Without suspecting our abode
Until we drive away.

How fair on looking back, the Day
We sauntered from the Door –
Unconscious our returning,
But discover it no more.

?   *1914*

549
(1660)

Glory is that bright tragic thing
That for an instant
Means Dominion –
Warms some poor name
That never felt the Sun,
Gently replacing
In oblivion –

?   *1914*

550
(1664)

I did not reach Thee
But my feet slip nearer every day
Three Rivers and a Hill to cross
One Desert and a Sea
I shall not count the journey one
When I am telling thee.

Two deserts, but the Year is cold
So that will help the sand

One desert crossed –
The second one
Will feel as cool as land
Sahara is too little price
To pay for thy Right hand.

The Sea comes last – Step merry, feet,
So short we have to go –
To play together we are prone,
But we must labor now,
The last shall be the lightest load
That we have had to draw.

The Sun goes crooked –
That is Night
Before he makes the bend.
We must have passed the Middle Sea –
Almost we wish the End
Were further off –
Too great it seems
So near the Whole to stand.

We step like Plush,
We stand like snow,
The waters murmur new.
Three rivers and the Hill are passed –
Two deserts and the sea!
Now Death usurps my Premium
And gets the look at Thee.

?   *1914*

551
(1666)
I see thee clearer for the Grave
That took thy face between

No Mirror could illumine thee
Like that impassive stone —

I know thee better for the Act
That made thee first unknown
The stature of the empty nest
Attests the Bird that's gone.

?

1955

552
(1669)

In snow thou comest —
Thou shalt go with the resuming ground,
The sweet derision of the crow,
And Glee's advancing sound.

In fear thou comest —
Thou shalt go at such a gait of joy
That man anew embark to live
Upon the depth of thee.

?

1955

553
(1672)

Lightly stepped a yellow star
To its lofty place —
Loosed the Moon her silver hat
From her lustral Face —
All of Evening softly lit
As an Astral Hall —
Father, I observed to Heaven,
You are punctual.

?

1914

554
(1677)

On my volcano grows the Grass
A meditative spot –
An acre for a Bird to choose
Would be the General thought –

How red the Fire rocks below –
How insecure the sod
Did I disclose
Would populate with awe my solitude.

? 1914

555
(1684)

The Blunder is in estimate.
Eternity is there
We say, as of a Station –
Meanwhile he is so near
He joins me in my Ramble –
Divides abode with me –
No Friend have I that so persists
As this Eternity.

? 1914

556
(1690)

The ones that disappeared are back
The Phoebe and the Crow
Precisely as in March is heard
The curtness of the Jay –

Be this an Autumn or a Spring
My wisdom loses way
One side of me the nuts are ripe
The other side is May.

?   *1914*

557
(1692)

The right to perish might be thought
An undisputed right –
Attempt it, and the Universe
Upon the opposite
Will concentrate its officers –
You cannot even die
But nature and mankind must pause
To pay you scrutiny.

(*1914*

558
(1695)

There is a solitude of space
A solitude of sea
A solitude of death, but these
Society shall be
Compared with that profounder site
That polar privacy
A soul admitted to itself –
Finite infinity.

?   *1914*

[312]

559
(1709)

With sweetness unabated
Informed the hour had come
With no remiss of triumph
The autumn started home

Her home to be with Nature
As competition done
By influential kinsmen
Invited to return –

In supplements of Purple
An adequate repast
In heavenly reviewing
Her residue be past –

? 1955

560
(1716)

Death is like the insect
Menacing the tree,
Competent to kill it,
But decoyed may be.

Bait it with the balsam,
Seek it with the saw,
Baffle, if it cost you
Everything you are.

Then, if it have burrowed
Out of reach of skill –
Wring the tree and leave it,
'Tis the vermin's will.

? 1896

561
(1725)

I took one Draught of Life –
I'll tell you what I paid –
Precisely an existence –
The market price, they said

They weighed me, Dust by Dust –
They balanced Film with Film,
Then handed me my Being's worth –
A single Dram of Heaven!

? 1929

562
(1726)

If all the griefs I am to have
Would only come today,
I am so happy I believe
They'd laugh and run away.

If all the joys I am to have
Would only come today,
They could not be so big as this
That happens to me now.

? 1945

563
(1732)

My life closed twice before its close –
It yet remains to see

If Immortality unveil
A third event to me

So huge, so hopeless to conceive
As these that twice befell.
Parting is all we know of heaven,
And all we need of hell.

?   1896

564
(1733)

No man saw awe, nor to his house
Admitted he a man
Though by his awful residence
Has human nature been.

Not deeming of his dread abode
Till laboring to flee
A grasp on comprehension laid
Detained vitality.

Returning is a different route
The Spirit could not show
For breathing is the only work
To be enacted now.

"Am not consumed," old Moses wrote,
"Yet saw him face to face" –
That very physiognomy
I am convinced was this.

?   1945

565
(1737)

Rearrange a "Wife's" affection!
When they dislocate my Brain!
Amputate my freckled Bosom!
Make me bearded like a man!

Blush, my spirit, in thy Fastness –
Blush, my unacknowledged clay –
Seven years of troth have taught thee
More than Wifehood ever may!

Love that never leaped its socket –
Trust entrenched in narrow pain –
Constancy thro' fire – awarded –
Anguish – bare of anodyne!

Burden – borne so far triumphant –
None suspect me of the crown,
For I wear the "Thorns" till *Sunset* –
Then – my Diadem put on.

Big my Secret but it's *bandaged* –
It will never get away
Till the Day its Weary Keeper
Leads it through the Grave to thee.

1945

566
(1739)

Some say goodnight – at night –
I say goodnight by day –
Good-bye – the Going utter me –
Goodnight, I still reply –

For parting, that is night,
And presence, simply dawn –
Itself, the purple on the height
Denominated morn.

? 1929

567
(1740)

Sweet is the swamp with its secrets,
Until we meet a snake;
'Tis then we sigh for houses,
And our departure take
At that enthralling gallop
That only childhood knows.
A snake is summer's treason,
And guile is where it goes.

? 1896

568
(1741)

That it will never come again
Is what makes life so sweet.
Believing what we don't believe
Does not exhilarate.

That if it be, it be at best
An oblative estate
This instigates an appetite
Precisely opposite.

? 1945

569
(1742)

The distance that the dead have gone
Does not at first appear –
Their coming back seems possible
For many an ardent year.

And then, that we have followed them,
We more than half suspect,
So intimate have we become
With their dear retrospect.

?   1896

570
(1743)

The grave my little cottage is,
Where "Keeping house" for thee
I make my parlor orderly
And lay the marble tea.

For two divided, briefly,
A cycle, it may be,
Till everlasting life unite
In strong society.

?   1896

571
(1745)

The mob within the heart
Police cannot suppress
The riot given at the first
Is authorized as peace

[318]

Uncertified of scene
Or signified of sound
But growing like a hurricane
In a congenial ground.

?

1945

572
(1755)

To make a prairie it takes a clover and one bee,
One clover, and a bee,
And revery.
The revery alone will do,
If bees are few.

?

1896

573
(1760)

Elysium is as far as to
The very nearest Room
If in that Room a Friend await
Felicity or Doom –

What fortitude the Soul contains,
That it can so endure
The accent of a coming Foot –
The opening of a Door –

c. 1882

1890

574
(1761)

A train went through a burial gate,
A bird broke forth and sang,
And trilled, and quivered, and shook his throat
Till all the churchyard rang;

And then adjusted his little notes,
And bowed and sang again.
Doubtless, he thought it meet of him
To say good-by to men.

?   *1890*

575
(1775)

The earth has many keys.
Where melody is not
Is the unknown peninsula.
Beauty is nature's fact.

But witness for her land,
And witness for her sea,
The cricket is her utmost
Of elegy to me.

?   *1945*

152-A
(398)

I had not minded – Walls –
Were Universe – one Rock –
And far I heard his silver Call
The other side the Block –

I'd tunnel – till my Groove
Pushed sudden thro' to his –
Then my face take her Recompense –
The looking in his Eyes –

But 'tis a single Hair –
A filament – a law –
A Cobweb – wove in Adamant –
A Battlement – of Straw –

A limit like the Veil
Unto the Lady's face –
But every Mesh – a Citadel –
And Dragons – in the Crease –

c. 1862   1929

Acknowledgments

The Poems of Emily Dickinson, from which this text derives, was made possible, first, by the gift of Gilbert H. Montague to Harvard University Library of funds for the purchase of the poet's manuscripts and other papers from the heirs to the literary estate, the late Alfred Leete Hampson and his wife Mary Landis Hampson; and second, by the courtesy of Millicent Todd Bingham in making available for study all of the large number of Dickinson manuscripts in her possession, later transferred by her to Amherst College.

This edition makes grateful and general acknowledgment to Harvard University Press and to Houghton Mifflin Company for permission to print here the Dickinson poems which are under copyright and have been published by them. The text is that of the variorum Harvard Edition (1955), as standardized in *The Complete Poems of Emily Dickinson* (Little, Brown and Company, 1960).

Thomas H. Johnson

Index of First Lines

Following the first lines of the poems are the page numbers.

It would have starved a gnat, 156
It's easy to invent a life, 182
Its hour with itself, 260
Its little ether hood, 293
It's such a little thing to weep, 21
I've dropped my brain — my soul is numb, 235
I've known a heaven like a tent, 30
I've seen a dying eye, 137

Jesus! thy crucifix, 28
Just lost, when I was saved, 16

Lay this laurel on the one, 282
Let down the bars, oh death, 238
Let me not mar that perfect dream, 275
Life and death and giants, 176
Light is sufficient to itself, 211
Lightly stepped a yellow star, 310
Like some old fashioned miracle, 54
Longing is like the seed, 265
Love is anterior to life, 220
Love is done when love's begun, 292
Love, thou art high, 108
Low at my problem bending, 8

Many a phrase has the English language, 41
March is the month of expectation, 284
Me, change! Me, alter, 39
Me from myself to banish, 165
Me prove it now, whoever doubt, 134
Mine by the right of the white election, 131
Mine enemy is growing old, 293
Much madness is divinest sense, 101
Must be a woe, 145
My cocoon tightens, colors tease, 245
My faith is larger than the hills, 190
My life closed twice before its close, 314
My life had stood, a loaded gun, 187
My period had come for prayer, 141
My triumph lasted till the drums, 261
Myself was formed a carpenter, 119

Nature affects to be sedate, 253
Nature and God — I neither knew, 208
"Nature" is what we see, 168
Nature sometimes sears a sapling, 60

Nature the gentlest mother is, 195
No bobolink reverse his singing, 188
No brigadier throughout the year, 298
No crowd that has occurred, 127
No man can compass a despair, 115
No man saw awe, nor to his house, 315
No other can reduce, 228
No rack can torture me, 88
None can experience stint, 191
Not any higher stands the grave, 265
Not probable — the barest chance, 75
Not with a club the heart is broken, 272

Of all the souls that stand create, 167
Of all the sounds despatched abroad, 63
Of bronze and blaze, 49
Of consciousness, her awful mate, 216
Of course I prayed, 85
Of God we ask one favor, 304
Of nearness to her sundered things, 153
Of silken speech and specious shoe, 216
Of tribulation these are they, 66
Oh sumptuous moment, 247
On a columnar self, 195
On my volcano grows the grass, 311
On the world you colored, 254
One and one are one, 191
One anguish in a crowd, 142
One crucifixion is recorded only, 139
One dignity delays for all, 9
One need not be a chamber to be haunted, 168
One of the ones that Midas touched, 289
Only a shrine, but mine, 220
Our journey had advanced, 157
Our share of night to bear, 10
Ourselves we do inter with sweet derision, 252
Out of sight? What of that, 175
Over and over, like a tune, 80
Over the fence, 33

Pain has an element of blank, 166
Papa above, 7
Pass to thy rendezvous of light, 299
Perception of an object costs, 240
Pink, small, and punctual, 274
Prayer is the little implement, 101
Presentiment is that long shadow on the lawn, 189